HOME

WORTHY

HOW TO BUY YOUR
DREAM HOME WITH EASE

SANDRA RINOMATO

◆ FriesenPress

Suite 300 - 990 Fort St
Victoria, BC, V8V 3K2
Canada

www.friesenpress.com

Copyright © 2020 by Sandra Rinomato
First Edition — 2020

Visit www.sandrarinomato.com and www.homeworthybook.com for more information about Sandra and the products and services she offers. Reach out to Sandra Rinomato at 1820 Bloor Street West, Toronto ON M6P 3K6 and via her websites, by phone at 416.565.3001

All rights reserved.

No part of this publication may be reproduced in any form, or by any means, electronic or mechanical, including photocopying, recording, or any information browsing, storage, or retrieval system, without permission in writing from FriesenPress.

This book is not intended to provide personalized legal, accounting, financial, investment, career, coaching or relationship advice. Readers are encouraged to seek the counsel of competent professionals with regard to such matters. The work and stories included is for your information and entertainment only, is based on the author's personal experiences and should not be misconstrued as professional advice. The Author and Publisher specifically disclaim any liability, loss or risk which is incurred as a consequence, directly or indirectly, of the use and application of any of the contents of this work.

While the Author has made best efforts to determine the source of all quotes contained herein, when a quote is attributed to more than one person the author has not included a definitive source.

Some names and identifying details have been changed to protect the privacy of individuals.

ISBN
978-1-5255-5532-9 (Hardcover)
978-1-5255-5533-6 (Paperback)
978-1-5255-5534-3 (eBook)

1. Self-Help, Motivational & Inspirational

Distributed to the trade by The Ingram Book Company

"YOU ARE HOME WORTHY! Buying a home is probably the biggest thing you'll ever do in your life, it certainly was for me. I think a lot of people make the assumption, that any money I've made over the years has been from the music business. On the contrary, buying and selling houses was a very big part of me forging ahead financially. I'll never forget the feeling of walking into the very first place I ever bought- it was 67,000 dollars. Honestly, it may have well been Ten million, but it felt glorious!

I knew I was doing something that would change how I felt about myself. I had a sense of pride and accomplishment and I knew that I was doing something great for my future self.

With her new book-Sandra Rinomato is giving us all the opportunity to invest and believe and cheer on our future selves. Her expertise is unparalleled and her advise is uncomplicated and easy to understand. Sandra has done it all, she's seen the markets rise and fall and rise again and she can show you how to become Home Worthy and truly live your best life."

—Jann Arden, Singer-Songwriter

Pat,
hope you enjoy!
Sandra

TABLE OF CONTENTS

DEDICATION

To the two women who drove me crazy by stopping one foot short of the finish line after years of planning your home purchase, I thank you. I needed to find out why you did that so I could show others how to achieve their dreams and avoid stopping short like you did. Hence the book was born and my true self became.

To my perfect mate, Gary, thank you for all of your support, for allowing me to dream, and for teaching me that I am worthy of you and of all good things.

For Angie

ACKNOWLEDGEMENTS

It's so difficult to pinpoint the exact moment I heard a thing for the first time, or when I heard it for the last time before I was finally inspired to take action on it. I'm so grateful for all of the people who have shared the positive messages that are readily available to billions of people now and have helped me become the woman I am. I'm especially grateful to the wise inner being that guides me moment by moment even when I refuse to listen. You are always there, always wise, always patient and always pure love. I'm grateful for every inspiring quote, video, chapter, sentence or being that ever sparked my desire to grow and to abandon the comfort of my conditioning.

I thank the people who have helped me on this book writing and publishing journey, starting with my husband Gary MacRae for always encouraging me to pursue my dreams even when it caused some discomfort or upheaval in our lives. You surpass my expectations of a great partner and I love you. Thank you Peggy McColl for your invaluable information about publishing and manifesting. To my contacts at FriesenPress thanks for your help and guidance. I'm very grateful to all of the creators, participants and fans of my TV shows for helping to make the shows successful, which allowed me to achieve my desire to help people in my own way.

Most of all, I thank each of you for reading this book, taking control of your own life and allowing yourself to dream and achieve all that you can. It took me decades to realize that I want to spend the rest of my life inspiring people to believe in themselves and their limitless capabilities. I am so thrilled that I continue to grow as a result of our interactions.

INTRODUCTION

I was the host of two real estate reality television shows called *Property Virgins* and *Buy Herself.* I learned so much from this segue in my real estate career and am very grateful for every lesson. Among many other things, I learned what the buyers were thinking and saying when I wasn't around! That was eye-opening. The truth is often shocking.

I created and pitched the show *Buy Herself,* which is about single women buying homes, about women taking control of their finances and their lives, about women stepping into their own power and living their best lives. Sadly, the show was given only one season from HGTV Canada, which I believe was a big mistake on their part but obviously I'm biased.

In real life, I continue to work with my favourite demographic, single women. I love that women are strong, independent, and fiscally responsible. In recent years I met and worked with two women independently who seemed to really have their act together and BAM! Each of them stopped one toe-length away from the finish line. Easily, they could have been on the podium but they fell lame. I had seen this happen many times before but I never quite understood what the heck had happened! I couldn't figure it out. It drove me nuts.

On paper, these women were strong, committed, determined, had saved money for years, and at the exact time when they could reach out and grab the brass ring they stopped themselves. Suddenly, each of these women pulled out of the race and wrote me very lengthy emails trying to convince me that they were right to do so. Or maybe they were trying to convince themselves, I don't know. But, I had to figure out what had really gone wrong. The excuses they gave me were not the true reasons, so I started digging.

At that same point in my life I rekindled my passion for self-development and *voila*! I had discovered the ONE THING that these women needed in order to be successful in buying their own homes. I had figured out the answer to the riddle. I realized that I had been using the ONE THING as well and that I could share this knowledge with you so you could avoid making the same costly mistakes. I had no choice but to write this book and create the online program. I embarked on the incredibly difficult journey of writing a book. Man, it's tough, but I hurled out my vision on these pages and with help from the right people who took it and polished it, here it is, ready for you to consume with or without wine. White goes best with this because you may begin sobbing and spill so let's stick to white wine for now, okay? Warning, this stuff may evoke an emotional response as you read these stories and learn what I consider to be the truth about women based on my own history and decades of working with women. On these pages, I share my insight on how we can make everything better for ourselves.

After visiting many of my clients a few months after they move in, they are pissed at themselves that they didn't do it sooner and have already started planning for another property to add to their portfolio. Yup, it can be addictive and for sure you will be a changed person once you read this book and achieve the goal of home ownership. You'll be changed for the best. I promise.

CHAPTER 1

Who Are the One in Four?

I began working in real estate in 1996 and in 2006 became the host of a real estate reality show called *Property Virgins*, the network's highest rated show. I completed 130 episodes with filming in Toronto and various U.S. cities and in 2011 decided to leave the show. You may think it's crazy to leave a number one show, but I just wasn't enjoying my life and work had become a grind. I woke up several mornings resenting having to go to work and felt that life was too short for that. I was exhausted. I wanted to get more joy back into my life.

I went back to selling homes as a real estate salesperson and upgraded my licensing to Broker status with intentions of opening up my own business. I accomplished the goal in 2011 and was enjoying life again. Real estate was truly my best fit and because I was no longer required to travel away from my home and family for five months of the year. I was able to reconnect with family and friends and to actually have control over how I spent my time.

Throughout my real estate career I had become aware of a statistic: one in four buyers is a single woman. This sounds fairly predictable. You would think that couples represent 50 per cent of buyers, women 25 per cent, and men 25 per cent. Not so! Only 10 per cent of buyers are single men.

So many questions arise: why aren't men buying at the same rate as women? What are men buying and spending their money on? Why don't they buy real estate? Why are so many women buying? When did this start? How does this fit with the stereotype of women being incapable of managing their money?

The sociologist in me was very intrigued by this information from the very first time I read it. Other realtors and the public just let it fly by them unaware of how interesting the times are. "May you live in interesting times" is an old Chinese curse, and I believe we do in fact live in very interesting times that involve change. I believe it is not a curse, but a blessing.

When I cite this statistic people ask, "Why are women buying real estate?" and my answer is, "Why ever not?" I remember when my aunt told me that she wasn't able to buy a condo in Hawaii in the '70s because she was a single woman. The builder wouldn't sell to her unless she had a male co-signer even though she had her own money, a job, and no expenses. I had heard that not long ago, women could never get credit even if they had careers. No credit cards, no car loans, no mortgages without a male co-signer. So what changed? Did the money become available first or did the demand come first?

I'm sure the demand was strong enough to cause the banks to identify an entirely new client base they could tap into. Women represent more than 50 per cent of the population! It's possible that women were subject to higher interest rates than their male counterparts and this may still be true today, as first of all they could get away with it and secondly it was perceived that lending to women would be riskier than lending to men, although there was no supporting data.

In 2011, I approached HGTV Canada, which had picked up *Property Virgins* back in 2006 and pitched a show I had created which was about women buying real estate on their own called *Buy Herself*. I wanted the show to explore the heart connection with these women and be more soulful than the previous show. HGTV picked it up for one season of 14 episodes. After we finished the season, I was told they were focusing on driving more male viewers to the network so they were green lighting male hosts and building shows so *Buy Herself* was not picked up again.

The women I worked with during my real estate career and the women on *Buy Herself* the TV show all had interesting stories. These women were not buying homes because they were getting married and wished to start a family, which is an absolutely wonderful reason to buy. But it should not be the only reason or a reason that you wait for. You don't need a reason to buy a home other than you want to.

I had been working with women who each wanted to buy homes. I found it odd when more than one of them pulled out at the very last minute. Each of them had planned, saved and worked toward buying real estate but something stopped them, and I wanted to know what it was. As I started to delve into the reasons why they had stopped their home search one inch away from success it became clear to me that it was because of the way they had approached their goal. The more I thought about it the more I began to understand what had truly happened. The more I researched, the more I helped myself. The more I helped myself the more I could help others. It's a cycle of contribution that feeds and empowers, and I love every minute of it.

My story

In 2004, I had open heart surgery to close an atrial septal defect I was born with, commonly referred to as a hole in the heart. The hole was too big for the balloon procedure, which would fill the hole with a balloon inserted up through the groin replacing the need for open heart surgery. We had tried the procedure, and it had failed. The doctors had to stop because my heart had been going into arrest. Open heart surgery was the only option for me and there was no getting out of it. Trust me, I looked for ways to avoid it. There were some complications during the surgery followed by more complications during my recovery that kept me in hospital for two weeks instead of the anticipated four days. I almost died a few times. I always say that the doctors did an amazing job and what they couldn't accomplish through medicine I managed to do through visualization and determination.

I visualized my husband, Gary – who at the time was my boyfriend – and his little boy, whom I loved, running on the beach with the glorious sun above. We were fit, strong, laughing, and then we'd fall to our knees and would joyfully hug each other. I focused on that dream for hours each day as I lay in the hospital bed. That dream gave me a reason to stay alive and healthy and I truly believe it worked in helping me overcome the challenges. I remember actually making a decision to survive and to be healthy. I imagined that I spoke to God and said, "If it fits the master plan I'd like to stay and love these boys." I envisioned placing my life in God's hands. I guess it fit the plan because here I am.

The odds for my survival were only about 30 per cent. I'm not sure when I heard this statistic but I believe it was well after I had had the surgery. The odds were that I'd die on the operating table or within the two weeks following. I am so grateful that I did not connect with that statistic because had I focused on it I would surely be dead. I mean this from the bottom of my patched heart.

"I would tell my story to anyone I knew who was sick so they could help themselves."

I promised myself that I would tell my story to anyone I knew who was sick so they could help themselves. I do this even if I don't know them well. I know that some people will scoff at the story and may think me foolish, but I'd rather brave their opinions of me than avoid telling my story and possibly missing the opportunity to help someone.

I had the surgery on June 1, 2004. That year, Friday, August 13, my father went in for a small procedure and suffered a stroke that paralyzed him and made it impossible for him to speak. For about a month or two he didn't know who I was. He could remember his life until about the year 1960 and knew he had two daughters but had no idea he had a third, me. Slowly, his memory came back to him while he was at a nursing home where he eventually died in 2006.

Just before he died, I began shooting *Property Virgins*. I told him I was going to be on TV but he never got to see an episode. He died in April 2006 while we were shooting the second episode of the first season. I know he would have been very proud. We shot 130 episodes in Toronto and various U.S. cities, splitting the time between the two countries. The show was a Canadian concept and the U.S. bought it after the fifth rough cut, which I'm told is very good. It wasn't long before the show became number one on the network. Nobody was more surprised than me.

I remember that it all began for me one day while I was a realtor minding my own business. I had been out on appointments and when I returned to the office I listened to a voice message from a guy named Danny. The message went like this: "Hi Sandra, my name is Danny. Please call me at 416-xxx-xxxx. Thanks." At that time of year, early fall, realtors would get tons of sales calls from people selling calendars and pens, fridge magnet calendars, and other promotional items so I figured it was a call about that and not a real estate call. A typical real estate call has some info, like "I want to buy a house or sell a house", or "I saw your ad for a certain property", or "I got your number from a client of yours" or something of that nature. This message was simply a name and a phone number so I was skeptical. I didn't want to get stuck on one of those sales calls, I didn't want to waste my time speaking to someone if I had no interest in what he was selling. Why waste his time and my time? So I decided I wasn't going to call.

Then a voice in my head said, "Don't be that person; don't be the realtor that people complain about. They tell how they called and the realtor never called back." I had built a great career on calling everyone back, so it started to nag at me. "Ok, I'll call, it'll go to voicemail anyway, and I'll hear the company name and then I can decide what to do." So I called Danny's number. A receptionist picked up the phone and said, "Production," and the phone started to leave my ear heading for the base so I could hang up. I thought, "See? It's a calendar printing house and I got the production line by mistake. I knew it!"

But as I was hanging up I felt bad, it was rude to just hang up (this is true, this all happened very quickly but it all happened) so I didn't hang up after all. I asked for Danny, and not very enthusiastically at that. I was acting like a teenager who didn't want to do some chore. I figured it would go to voicemail, so I was very surprised when Danny actually answered the phone. What? Who answers the phone these days! Ugh! In the teenager voice, slightly less petulantly, "Hi Danny, this is Sandra, you called?" and then the direction of my life changed.

Danny told me they were filming a new show about first-time buyers. They were going to follow the buyers around documentary style as they bought their first home. I exclaimed, "Who on earth would watch that?" and I meant it. At that time, there was one other real estate show and I had watched it once or twice. I had participated in one episode; the show was *Buy Me*. I wasn't a huge fan of the show, but to be honest, in those days I hadn't been watching much TV. So I couldn't imagine the huge beast that reality real estate TV would become. I really thought that nobody would watch a show like that. Clearly I knew nothing about making TV.

Go for it, babe! You're a natural!

Danny laughed a bit, and then proceeded to tell me they were looking for a realtor to be part of the show and they would like to audition me. I hemmed and hawed, and he talked me into it. He said it would be a quick trip to Spadina Avenue for an interview and possibly a test reel. I agreed and then told Gary, my partner. He was extremely supportive and had so much faith in me. "Go for it, babe! You're a natural!"

So off I went on a drizzly day, hair spreading out into a frizzy triangle by the minute, wearing a clingy white sweater, which one does not do on TV unless you are seriously underweight and wish to appear heavier, which did not apply here. Sophia and Danny and I chatted a bit, on camera. Then they asked if we could pretend to be looking at a condo, the office we were in would serve as the condo, and they would pretend to be the buyers. They told me they wanted a work-live situation with a good address for business. I told them that Spadina Avenue was a well-known commercial street in the city and that the space offered old world charm with exposed brick walls, which were becoming very trendy at the time.

She complained about the view, and I recall saying something snarky, like, "What do you want, the view or the address? With your budget you can't have both. You want a view? I'll sell you a waterfront condo. You want work-live with an address, this is a great option." Then I looked up and saw the original wood tongue and groove ceiling and lost my mind on how beautiful it could be, the potential in it and how high the ceilings were, and I became very excited. Sophia and Danny looked at each other with a knowing look and told me they'd be in touch. That was October 2005.

In January 2006, I met up with some friends who were also in the local real estate business and heard that many of them had been called in for the same show. I had given up any hope of a callback, and it came as no surprise that they were still casting for it. Obviously, they weren't interested in hiring me, and I put it out of my mind.

One month later, in February, I was standing in slush in my heels at the bottom of my driveway with my partner, Gary, when I received a call from a man with a very low voice and British accent. He identified himself as the a member of the production team of the show and asked if I remembered auditioning for it. It wasn't like I was pursuing a career in TV so I wasn't auditioning for anything at that time. This show was the only one I had ever auditioned for.

He mentioned that his first task had been to review each of the audition reels. They were now calling some people back in for another audition and wanted to know if I was interested. Now, keep in mind, my partner had been a model and actor, and he told me tales of cattle calls where hundreds of people would show up and wait for their chance to audition, and I had heard that so many realtors had auditioned for the show. Furthermore, my dad was quite ill at this time, and I just didn't have the desire to start something new right then. On top of that, I wasn't interested in being on TV. So I told him thanks but no thanks, I was not interested in going back in for a second audition.

You can't imagine the shock in his voice! In show business nobody said no to a second audition; in fact they dreamed of receiving such a call. Gary was telling me to go for it! I was standing in slush in February in high-heeled shoes and wasn't interested in pursuing the conversation. The voice on the phone was flabbergasted. He tried to convince me to come in and although I hated to be rude I just wasn't into it. He pushed for a reason why not, and I asked how many people he had coming in. He was put off, I mean nobody in TV talked this way! They'd be jumping up and down with excitement! He answered, a little put off, that possibly five or six were invited back. I had been imagining the cattle calls and I said, "hundred?!" He must have thought I was insane. He explained, very slowly that only five or six people were being asked back for another audition. I was silent. This was unbelievable to me. I needed time to process it all. Gary was pushing me, "Go babe, go for it! You got this!" He was so excited for me. Honestly, if he hadn't been there when I got the call things would have been very different.

So the deep British voice on the other end of the line said, "We'll need you to come in on Thursday or Friday this week, as we need to start production on this ASAP." Okay, well another NO. I was headed out to San Francisco the very next day for my first ever real estate conference. It was the 100-year celebration for the real estate franchise I worked for at the time, and I had convinced a few of my friends to go. We were set to leave Toronto the very next day, February 14, 2006 and return the following Sunday. I had to turn down the British man once again. He told me not to go on my trip. I laughed! I wasn't going to cancel my trip and disappoint my friends for a "maybe" nor for something I didn't even want! He was shocked. I was shocked that he was shocked.

Then, suddenly, his voice went up two octaves, and he lost the British accent, "OMG, you're going to the convention! You must know my friend" and he named his friend. I did know of her, she was a top producer in the country and worked about one hour from Toronto. "Oh you'll have to tell her that we spoke and ask her all about the show, she knows about it! Okay, go and we'll wait for you! We'll audition you next week."

So off I went to San Francisco. At that time I had a Blackberry phone and received my emails on it unless my computer was on in which case the email would bypass the phone and go straight to the computer. While I was away, drinking and partying with thousands of realtors, an email came in from the producer, "Hurry home, it's between you and one other, and I'm pushing for you!" but I completely missed the email as it bypassed my Blackberry.

Don't do it!

My friend Robert was a top producing agent who had also gone to San Francisco. He called to ask where I was and invited me to the lobby of his hotel to have champagne with, you guessed it, the agent the series producer had mentioned. So off I went to sip champers with the best agents in Canada. I told her what was going on, and she immediately said, "Don't do it!" That was all I needed to once again talk me out of auditioning for the role. She explained that the show was going to have a television host and that the realtor would come in as an expert and would be onscreen for 2–3 minutes to explain the features of the house, the location and so on. She said that TV took so long to shoot and it would waste so much of my time for nothing. I was confused because the series producer had kept calling it a host position but she assured me it was only a short "expert" type stint. Once again I was convinced that my decision to turn down the audition and the opportunity was sound.

I arrived home late Sunday night to a voicemail that said my father was very ill and that I should go to the nursing home as soon as possible. I left a message for my assistant to contact the production company and tell him that my dad was dying and I'd be unavailable for who knows how long. Thanks but no thanks, you'd better find someone else.

I arrived at the nursing home only to find my father sitting up in bed barking orders at the nurses, in seemingly fine health for someone in his condition. I was the one who was suffering. I was jet lagged and hung over and plain old exhausted after the 100-year celebration. My dad was fine and whatever had ailed him had mysteriously disappeared.

In those days, you were required to turn off your phones when you entered the nursing home as it interfered with the medical equipment. I had left my phone in the car and when I turned it on again I saw that I had a message from the production company. He said that he understood the gravity of the situation, but I really had to come in for the audition. Um, clearly he did not understand the gravity of the situation as he had been told that my father was dying so I was a little put off. Gary said, "That's the business, babe, welcome to the business."

They arranged to have Sophia come over to meet me at my house. While I was getting ready I played around with my hair and was trying out a new cute hair flip that my stylist had given me the week before. My bangs weren't quite right so I fished about in my big box of hair tricks and I found a cute little brush I had completely forgotten about. I rolled up my bangs very tightly in this wooden brush that was about as thick as my ring finger. I gave it a couple of shots of hairspray, the kind you could practically hang wallpaper with and then I hit with the hair dryer on high heat. That was just enough to secure the brush in my hair, painfully digging its spikes into my scalp, never to be removed.

Talk about a really bad hair day

I panicked. I couldn't get the brush out of my hair. I tried pulling to the point of tears, I tried to pull hair out one at a time but it was so tightly wound up that it wouldn't budge. I didn't know what to do. I could hear Gary on the phone downstairs talking to a client. I ran to my laptop on the dining table passing the glass front door wearing only my bra and undies, freaking out because Sophia was going to arrive in mere minutes. I banged out an email to Gary, subject line, COME TO BATHROOM ASAP with no other content to the message. I waited. I was sweating. I heard Gary end the telephone conversation. I knew he'd come running to my aid any second now.

I waited. And waited. After what I was sure was an eternity I yelled, "GARY!" He came upstairs, and I told him what was happening. He laughed. I said "OK, laugh, it is funny, but help me. What am I going to do?" Then he bent over. I didn't know what he was doing. I thought maybe he had an idea. When he straightened up I saw that he was barely breathing from laughing so hard. But then he realized I was serious and this was really happening. I guess the look on my face, the sweat trickling down my body was sobering enough to make him focus.

Well, long story short, we didn't come up with a solution other than to cut the brush out of my bangs leaving one centimetre of hair at my hairline straight across my forehead. I looked like someone who was missing their two front teeth. My bangs were an integral part of my hairstyle and although I tried to comb over it to hide the obvious gap of missing hair it was to no avail. It was hideous.

When Sophia showed up at the door, I told her she may as well go home as I had had a hair accident. Very professionally, she pretended not to notice and with tilted head simply said, "Oh yes, I thought something was different about your hair. No, we aren't cancelling, we are going to go ahead with it." I was mortified.

We did the audition, the network finally agreed to hire me as host, not just the expert and the production company offered me the position. When I discovered what the pay was I was not interested in going any further. The pay was too low. I knew the amount of my time the show would require was going to ruin my real estate practice. I had a mature business that I had worked very hard to build. I was not prepared to give it up. Once again I turned it down. They upped the ante a bit and with Gary supporting me I finally agreed to sign the contract to become the host of *Property Virgins*. I agreed because I figured they would fire me soon anyway, or the show would get cancelled and it would be a nice memory. At least I'd have a few tapes to show my future grandchildren.

Property Virgins came out in the top five shows, then moved to top three and then number one on the network within a very short period of time. As I said earlier, nobody was more surprised than me.

I learned a lot when I watched the episodes of *Property Virgins* because I would see rational people break down into ugly crying as soon as the slightest obstacle appeared. This didn't usually happen when I was around during normal real estate showings but it was all caught on camera and when I saw it I was floored! I had no idea that these people were so broken by the slightest bump in the road. I wondered why this was happening and began to understand that their stories, their belief systems were causing a lot of friction for them.

In the next chapters we discuss our stories and how they affect us in our day-to-day lives and with real estate specifically.

CHAPTER 2

There Isn't Anyone You Couldn't Love if You Heard Their Story

Many people, including Mr. Rogers, are credited with having said that. I'm writing it here because I believe it too.

So many people have written to me over the years to say they empathize with me and give me great credit for keeping my cool when I would meet a Property Virgin they felt was difficult. I was actually surprised by that for many reasons. I was grateful for the positive feedback and loved that people could appreciate the difficulty that a good realtor faces when dealing with certain personalities. But I felt bad for the people they were talking about.

Everyone acts and reacts a certain way because of their story, their conditioning, their belief system. These beliefs are so ingrained in us that we really truly believe we are acting rationally and that we control our own thoughts. I feel bad for the people on TV who others love to criticize because I know they could learn to choose to react differently and by doing so could achieve their real estate dreams. Those people are judged on the behaviour that is based on conditioned beliefs, and I feel that is pretty unfair.

When you're in the hot seat you're stressed and may begin to create obstacles that do not exist in order to justify quitting on your goal. When we watch them on TV we are simply observers and because we're not in the hot seat at that moment we can recognize the folly of their false beliefs. It's much easier to recognize conditioned responses when you are calm and not anxious. Once the home buyers recognize their false beliefs and dismiss them they are able to move forward, achieve their goal of home ownership, and successfully purchase their dream home. It takes awareness, the freedom to dream, commitment to a goal, action, and determination.

"It takes awareness, the freedom to dream, commitment to a goal, action, and determination."

What would you say if I told you that our minds are making all of those beliefs up in order to keep us down? Your deep-rooted beliefs that have developed over the entirety of your life cause you to see obstacles where there are none. They come from your egoic mind. The function of the egoic mind is to keep you safe and whenever you want to do something unsafe it becomes the voice in your head that tells you to stop. It comes in very handy when you're approaching the edge of a steep two-hundred-foot drop at the edge of a cliff. It's designed for that purpose but it also keeps you back from really striving for your dreams. It tells you that you aren't capable, you are not deserving, you shouldn't try to be better than everyone else, you should be content with the way things are, this is how it's always been done, and so many more false ideas. You believe these are your own thoughts but they are the thoughts you were taught to believe by a society, culture, and family that were operating from their conditioned beliefs known as paradigms.

Let me explain how that works. When you are a little girl in an Italian-Canadian household in the 1960s there is a good chance you are being conditioned to be an underachiever by today's standards. You are being groomed to be a good wife and mother using the definition of good wife that falls within your family's belief system. You are congratulated for good grades in school but not encouraged to pursue a career, or a university degree or two. Your brother's lesser grades are celebrated and he's encouraged to be an entrepreneur or a doctor . . . the sky's the limit. He's not groomed to be a good husband and father because it's less important and not even "a thing". Boys were raised to be the breadwinners and girls were raised to be good wives following years of tradition that dictated what that looked like. There was pressure on both sexes to fulfill their functions and to do it without question.

You think you're making choices but . . .

In that scenario, kids are not encouraged to find a career path that makes them happy. As a girl you are not conditioned, trained, or encouraged to find a career path that makes you happy. As a matter of fact you aren't really trained to pursue happiness at all. You are told that everything will be fine as long as you become a good wife and mother. Your beliefs are conditioned, you are conditioned, your ego is conditioned. You think you're making choices, but you aren't. You are a well-trained pet.

It's nobody's fault, per se, your parents are only doing what they believe is the best thing for you. That belief is based on their experiences growing up with traditions and what they were taught. So when your marriage falls apart even though you fit the mold of a good wife you start to question those beliefs – if you're one of the lucky ones. Although I don't have any brothers, my upbringing followed along those lines.

You deserve to be happy!

I married the first time in 1996, with faith that my husband would be smarter than I was, more financially/fiscally responsible than I was, and would follow the rules I learned as a child. When that proved not to be the case I began to second guess everything my family had taught me. I can tell you it was quite a ride. The entire belief system and the foundation of everything I believed came crashing down and crumbled beneath my feet. As difficult as it was I couldn't be more grateful for that excruciatingly trying time. It gave me the right, the nerve to create my own beliefs with tenacity. I had tried it their way, and it had failed. I hadn't failed, the system had failed me. Now I was free to try my own system, to make myself happy. What? Happy? Who in the heck told you that you deserve to be happy?

Only one person did and when I first heard it my head started to spin as if I had vertigo, so I suppressed it and moved onto the steadier ground I had grown up on. That was safer and better for me, or so I thought.

This happened when I was going to pack up and move out east to Moncton, N.B. to be with the guy I was dating while he trained to be a pilot. He later became my first husband. My older cousin said, "That's nice that you are supporting his goals, but what about you, what do you want to do?" Those simple words, that simple question threw me completely off balance. I hadn't ever thought of it before, not really. I had earned an Honours degree in Sociology at University of Toronto but I never pursued a worthy career. I was stuck in the belief that if I became a good wife everything would be great and I'd live a good life so I didn't have to worry about my career. I hadn't been raised with ideas of pursuing my own career and never thought I should so I continued working in retail, which was comfortable because I had done it for years. I worked my way up the ranks a bit, not too far of course. Becoming the CEO was not aligned with my beliefs at that time.

You might ask why I bothered getting a degree. Here's the deal. I was an honour student in high school. I was in the special class for browners, which is an eighties term that we called smart kids. It was short for brown-nosers. I'll just leave the rest to your imagination. It was a degrading term to the ones who used it against you but I never thought of it that way. It meant we were smart and if people wanted to believe that we kissed butt to get the marks I knew they were wrong so I didn't care. I enjoyed some accolades at school but I never let them go to my head. I under-achieved on purpose because academic achievement wasn't something that was widely applauded at home so why should I bother? I knew I could get really good grades because I had already done so in Grade 9. I had been afraid that high school was going to be very difficult so I really applied myself that first year. I didn't want to fail because that just didn't jive with my perception of myself, thankfully. Once I had proved to myself that I could get marks in the nineties, I worked toward grades of just 75–85 per cent. Ultimately, I didn't want

to challenge the status quo at home where the culture was non-supportive of my academic career.

"My success at school allowed a tiny little
seed of self-esteem to be planted."

At school, I was applauded and recognized as being above average
but at home I was not. I figured my family knew me much better than
the teachers did. It was easier to believe that I was only slightly above
average than to believe that I could and should be one of the very top
students in the school. If my marks came in at a slightly higher than
average mark I could walk the line between the two beliefs quite comfortably. Thank goodness for my success at school because that allowed
a tiny little seed of self-esteem to be planted.

Back to why I went to university. When I was in Grade 12, David
Letterman landed a morning show. Many people don't know this about
his career but he was the freshest, funniest thing to happen to morning
television. That year the high school changed our schedule to a two-day
schedule with only four periods per day. Instead of having all eight
classes every day you'd have four longer periods on Day 1 and a different four subjects on Day 2. Because I was a browner I had gotten all of
my credits, which left me with a spare period first thing on Day 2. I had
dreamed of being able to sleep in, dreamed of having a spare first period
ever since I heard tell of it during Grade 9. I was stoked! And when I discovered this David Letterman guy on morning TV, I was even happier.
Every other weekday I would have my breakfast of champions, coffee
with milk and Italian "S cookies" or half a bag of Chocolate Chips Ahoy
to dunk while I watched this incredibly funny guy on TV.

In my recollection of this experience, my mom found me in the family
room on a school day with the TV on at 9:00 AM she freaked. I tried
to explain about the new schedule but she truly believed I was skipping
classes, that I was being lazy and told me to get a job as a secretary
and marry my boss. In retrospect she may have been half kidding, but

I gravitated to the limiting belief, as was my habit, and believed I was limited in my abilities. A belief is just a thought you keep thinking and you attract more of it to you. You fail to see the event, comment, thing that contradicts the thought and you only see what you believe. In my mom's statement I only recognized the part that limited me. I chose to internalize the portion that was aligned with my belief and was comfortable, the one that allowed me to shrink myself into my comfort zone. For the record, being a secretary was a decent job but the point is that the limiting belief was mine to cling to or to reject.

I believed that becoming a secretary and marrying my boss was my fate, all that I was good for because my mom said so. As my boss and future husband I envisioned a short greasy Hush Puppies-clad man with his polyester pants pulled up above his belly button, sweat stains under his arms and a horrible greasy comb over hairstyle standing with his hands on his hips admonishing me for something. The vision terrified me and I immediately decided to procrastinate by completing Grade 13, an extra year at high school so I could put off my fate for one more year. In Ontario, Grade 13 was an optional year that was only required to get into university. You could enroll in community college with your Grade 12 and if you were going to work right out of high school you didn't need any more than Grade 12. I figured, if that was my fate I'd procrastinate by going to school for one more year, and I'd even apply to university. I wasn't allowed to leave home to go to university out of Toronto. My dad said there were three perfectly good schools in Toronto and if I was not accepted to one of those universities I should get a job or apply to college.

Limiting beliefs – limiting behaviour

Because of my limiting beliefs or paradigms, I didn't really believe I'd get accepted at university and so I didn't even consult with the guidance counsellor to learn about the process or to ensure that I was applying to the proper campuses. I put in my three choices, one of which didn't even make sense as it was a law school. I was shocked when I was accepted to U of T Erindale campus and off I went, knowing full well that they would discover I was a fraud and would expel me in a humiliating and public way. Of course that never happened but I made sure my grades weren't amazing by agreeing to work 32 hours per week. Managing a busy store provided me with an excuse for when I would fail. I was managing a store at a big mall during the time I was enrolled at U of T full time. I would have worked more hours at the store but I seem to recall that the company would only give me 32 hours per week in order to keep me as a part-time employee. My understanding is that if they gave me more hours they'd have to increase my wages and give me benefits as a full-timer. I knew it wasn't fair but I let them do it because I believed I wasn't worthy of more. That was but one of my many limiting beliefs.

It was senseless to sabotage myself in school and elsewhere. I regret it now as I look back with a clear understanding and I am grateful that I was able to break free from the habit of self-sabotage. Can I tell you something though? It's common. This kind of sabotage is very real and just about everyone sabotages their success one way or another. In these chapters, I will share stories of women who have allowed their conditioned responses to hold them back from success as I will also share stories of women who control their own thoughts and lives.

The push out of your comfort zone

Back to those Property Virgins you love to yell at while watching the show. It's not really their personalities that you react to. It is their subconscious minds that cause the behaviour that you object to. Their actions are predictable as they follow a pattern. These kids are just are victims of their conditioning the same way you and I are.

Your thoughts, the things you believe in and would even bet your life on don't belong to you. They are triggered by people or situations, they are triggered by conditioning, a past experience. Things you were taught to believe will haunt you for life unless you shed light on them and take steps to get rid of them. These include things that society teaches you both subliminally and overtly. The more something challenges your identity the more strongly you will avoid it. It causes anxiety because it is trying to push you out of your comfort zone. I'll teach you how to meet these false beliefs head on and get rid of them. It takes courage to follow your true desires and although I may not know you and may never meet you I know you possess the stuff that it takes.

In the following chapters I will help you understand the difference between the truth and what you were led to believe. You were led to believe many things just as a horse is led by the bit in his mouth. A horse is stronger than anyone reading this sentence and could gain his freedom at any time but he chooses not to because of the conditioning that forces him to accept his circumstance.

The good news is that you can take the bit out of your mouth. You don't have to accept those beliefs any longer. You can create new experiences and new responses to stimuli that trigger the old beliefs. You can create a whole new reality, one that you want deeply and honestly. You can become a whole new person with renewed energy and vigour, with more love in your life and all of the wonderful things that you can dream of.

You may be reading this book because you are considering buying a property. It could be your first home or it could be an investment property. You will most likely encounter some obstacles along the way home. I hope to empower you with skills and the mindset to overcome and conquer any obstacles that may impede your success.

"You must be determined to achieve the
goal of home ownership or you will fail."

I met a woman named Lily who came in to talk to me about buying real estate. She had been living with various roommates over the years and her current roomie had decided to move out. Lily had decided that it was finally time to get a place on her own. She wasn't quite sure if she should rent or if she should buy. She had made the decision to move out on her own but had not yet decided if she would buy her own place.

I stopped the conversation right there. I'm all about real estate home ownership and I believe that it is the best investment in the world. I believe everyone should own real estate either to live in or to rent out as an investment. When I heard that she wasn't sure if she should stay within her comfort zone by renting or if she should begin the process of buying I knew that the many obstacles that would come her way during the buying process would send her running. I told her that if she didn't really want it, need it, think about it all the time, she'd end up renting anyway and she should just recognize the fact right then. I told her I'd be thrilled to help her should she decide to buy once she's thought it over. She never called again.

Now, she may have been pissed off at me for speaking to her that way, but in reality, I was only foretelling her future for her own benefit. You cannot succeed in buying real estate in Toronto if you are wishy washy because it's far too challenging! It's very competitive, each situation is different, there is no cookie-cutter process and you must be determined to achieve the goal of home ownership or you will fail. There are too many decisions to make, too many naysayers whose opinions will convince you to alter your course and oftentimes you would be forced to make a decision on the fly with no time to deliberate. I mean it's tough! So to sit there and say you aren't sure if you want to buy I know what the answer is going to be. If there is a shadow of a doubt about wanting to buy real estate in Toronto you'd be wasting your time if you tried in that state of mind.

Lily's motivation was to be on her own, which was already outside the box thinking for her. She did not have a strong motivation or desire to buy a home at that time and therefore she did not have the goal to become a homeowner. I wanted to prevent her from failing because that one failure could become the reason why she would hold herself back for years to come, and not just with real estate but with every aspect of her life. She was prepared to take baby steps, which is totally fine. She wanted to play small and that's not a problem; she could go at her own pace or perhaps she would not play at all. For the average person, hassles and obstacles are good enough reasons to play small or not at all.

Faith is the only antidote to failure

Belief is a state of mind and faith is the only antidote to failure. A committed person knows that life is full of obstacles and challenges and that obstacles are part of life, part of success. How do you deal with challenges? What is your habit? Do you overcome your obstacles or do your obstacles overcome you? The practise of constantly overcoming challenges will force you to grow to a point where any challenge becomes easy. If you don't confront and overcome the obstacles, you are developing and reinforcing the habit of being stopped by obstacles. You are conditioning yourself to fail. You are perpetuating the belief that you cannot succeed. When you say you can't do it you allow the obstacle to be bigger than you. If you won't do it, you are lying to yourself based on your beliefs. You believe something that is nonsense. You are allowing the external circumstance to control your inside self, your true self. You can start living from the inside out instead of the outside in and you will be happy, healthy, and wealthy. I say this with conviction because I know this to be true.

"Start living from the inside out instead of the outside in and you will be happy, healthy, and wealthy."

The more time and effort it takes to achieve a goal the more room there is for the habit of procrastination to set in. Without the instant rush and biochemical change you experience from a win, the reward seems more and more unattainable. All of the old habits come back and all of the paradigms come in to sabotage your success. Achieving a goal quickly allows the average person to maintain the necessary level of emotion in order to achieve the goal. It's much harder to be consistent when you don't see immediate results.

When you set the goal of home ownership or any goal, it should become a burning desire in you that can only be extinguished with success. It should be in the back of your mind all day every day. It should be top of mind awareness. Let's say you were to go to a movie at the theatre, you're engrossed in the film, and you're enjoying yourself. On the screen comes a scene where someone is driving down a city street and you notice the condos in the scene. Your attention is drawn towards it and you rekindle your desire and commitment to purchase real estate. Your mind may wander a bit and you may not pay attention to what happens next onscreen. A few months ago, before you made the decision to work toward your goal of homeownership, you would have watched the scene and would not have paid much attention to any of the housing on screen. If there was something extraordinary like a mansion or a fabulous penthouse overlooking the city you may have tuned in to it because it was part of the storyline, and it was out of the ordinary. Otherwise, the houses and condos would have gone by virtually unnoticed.

Lily did not have the desire yet, she had not committed to home ownership over all else, and her home search would have seen challenges that she would not have been equipped to deal with. Failing would have reinforced the belief that she could not do it, which in turn would hold her back from ever trying again. Those obstacles would continue to reappear in her life and each time they appeared they would be tougher and bigger.

Self-sabotage is a form of self-punishment

For many reasons, some people stop one centimetre short of the finish line and always will until something changes. They may be in the habit of not allowing themselves to win, not allowing themselves to complete what they have started. They may be in the habit of self-sabotage without knowing it. Self-sabotage is a form of self-punishment and the habit started in them ages ago.

At about this point, you may be asking yourself why a realtor would write about self-development. Besides the fact that I've loved the subject for years, real estate is a people business and you learn an awful lot about people and what makes them behave the way they do. I help people by solving their real estate problems. Sometimes their problem is that they want a million dollar home but they can't get their hands on the money. Other clients have access to the money but their problem is that they can't find a home they want to buy. Sometimes the problem is that they think they want to buy a house but truly they don't. This last scenario has occurred so many times in my career that I decided to find out why this is. I share my findings with you in these pages. I hope that the stories and information in this book will help you recognize your own limiting beliefs so that you can set and achieve your goal of home ownership and all of your dreams.

Later on in this book you'll read Sydney's story, and you will see what a warrior can accomplish and how important persistence is to help you achieve your goal. You'll read Fatima's story and virtually feel her commitment to create a better life for herself. There are so many more stories that will inspire and some that will reveal some hidden truths about you that as yet you have no awareness of. You'll learn how to value yourself enough to put your attention on the life you want to lead. I hope your journey will bring you to fulfillment each day and for life.

John C. Maxwell said, "Life is a matter of choices and every choice you make makes you." What choices do you make and which version of you are you creating? Stick with me, I have a lot more to say and I will show you how this all relates to real estate. I promise.

CHAPTER 3

Why Women Buy Homes

I felt it was important to get the male perspective on buying real estate and to try to understand what was going on in the psyche of men who bought and those who didn't. I asked many people why men were not buying real estate at the same rate as women.

Many times, the initial reaction was to state that men have a greater fear of commitment than women do and they don't want to commit to a property. It's an old cliché and an updated version of that paradigm is referred to as the fear of missing out (FOMO). FOMO does not just relate to the need to be constantly connected via social media, it is also defined as a fear of regret, having missed out on a more profitable investment or some great experience. These men worry that a better option may become available later on, or that they may want to use their cash for something else, or they may want to move to a different part of the city, country, or the world and would not want to be strapped down by home owner-ship. These men want to be free to do as they please without being tied down. Men feel little or no pressure to buy real estate before they have a committed relationship and feel that they will only need to buy once that happens. Right now, they want to be the rolling stone that gathers no moss. While it may be true of some men, please note that I've watched as women who thought they wanted to buy a home feared the commitment so it is not exclusively male, however single men in general do not share the same beliefs as the women when it comes to owning property.

Many women invest in one of the best investments in the world as the subconscious expression of freedom and individual power. Their individual power allows women to rise above and act on the belief that they don't need what society tells them they need in order to make their way in the world. They know they don't need a partner by their side. They know they can do it alone. They have the power to choose their lives and to create their own wealth and their own reality.

Some women perceive that their earning potential is limited and use real estate as a means to provide that extra bit of wealth. Statistics Canada data indicate that more than 75 per cent of Canada's national wealth comes from real estate and about 72 per cent according to the U.S. Federal Reserve.[1] Let that sink in a while. How would that affect you should you become a lifelong tenant? In these pages lies the story of a woman who I refer to as the spokesperson for home ownership. A woman who was not worried that her career had come to an abrupt end because she had only two remaining mortgage payments to make before she owned her home outright. If she had been renting, the circumstances would have been much more stressful. She had built wealth and options for herself through property.

Some women feel defensive about being single when their male counterparts do not. They ask, "What if Mr. Right comes along?" Some women would pull this one out near the beginning of their journey and it often keeps them from even starting. They worried that as soon as they purchased a home they would meet Mr. Right. So what's the problem? You're allowed to date when you own real estate. It's a snarky rhyming response to an absolutely intolerable question. Would you want a partner who would be threatened by your success? To a strong success-conscious man you would be no less attractive simply because you had your act together. Would you shrink yourself to make sure he feels bigger than he does now or bigger than you? Would you knowingly limit yourself this way? You might get the guy but would that truly serve you? Do you want to live a life where you are not allowed to thrive, where your happiness depended on staying in the shadows for the sake

---

1   Jesse Ferreras, "76% of Canada's national wealth is wrapped up in
     real estate", December 19, 2018. https://globalnews.ca/news/4775685/
     canada-national-wealth-real-estate

of someone else's ego? Or would you want someone who loves you for your true self? Do you want a man who only wants a needy female so he can feel needed and his ego will be mollified? Or would you be attracted to a man who would encourage you to be all that you could be?

Women are often afraid to be powerful. Let's use a stage term and let's find our light. This amazing quote by Marianne Williamson is something we should all repeat on daily basis and in doing so we'd all be different in a significant and positive way.

> Our deepest fear is not that we are inadequate.
> Our deepest fear is that we are powerful beyond measure.
> It is our Light, not our darkness that most frightens us.
>
> We ask ourselves, Who am I to be brilliant, gorgeous, talented, fabulous? Actually, who are we not to be?
>
> You are a child of God. Your playing small does not serve the world. There is nothing enlightened about shrinking so that other people do not feel insecure around you. We were born to manifest the Glory of God that is within us. It is not just in some of us, it is in everyone.
>
> And as we let our light shine, we unconsciously give other people permission to do the same. As we are liberated from our own fears, our presence automatically liberates others.
>
> **—Marianne Williamson**

My interpretation is that she describes how we believe we are afraid of the darkness but in truth we are afraid to shine. She goes further to say that by allowing ourselves to flourish and by allowing our brilliance to shine for all to see we in turn allow others, actually encourage the freedom to be their true selves. Imagine how the human race would advance with this new paradigm.

"Move forward with your life plans and keep your heart open to all opportunities."

My advice is to move forward with *your* life plans and keep your heart open to all opportunities. There is no need to hold back. Live your life now; you are whole as you are. You are not half a woman, you are complete. You possess everything you need already. You do not need to live up to anyone else's expectations of you. Don't obsess over the label "single, unattached". It does not mean that you are not worthy, or not loveable. You don't have to wait to be fixed because are perfect right now. Happy people live who they are *right now.*

Women who are afraid to become homeowners just in case Mr. Right comes along cling to an outdated culture from the past that does not serve them well. As some people show an unwillingness to release the old culture we experience friction as it rubs up against our new reality. The past and the present have not yet found their meeting point. Let go of the dinosaur and embrace your new reality, the one you create for yourself by following the steps in this book.

We put the cap on our own heads

Women are buying real estate for many other reasons such as a desire to build wealth, a desire known as nesting, for instant credibility, and preparing for their futures.

Women feel that their income is capped and that they will be looked over for the top positions in their organization. Perhaps that is why 25 per cent of all buyers are single women and only 10 per cent are single men. Men don't feel the need to supplement their income the way women do. Men know they will get the top positions and top earnings while women believe they will not get the job or the money, and they appreciate the opportunity to build wealth that home ownership provides them.

> "Women, blow your own horn because
> nobody else is going to do it for you."

Why don't women get to be top dog? Some say it's because women focus on their jobs and not their careers. They do the job extremely well, perhaps much better than their male counterpart, but the man plays the game. He focuses on his career rather than the job, and he gains a favourable reputation with the decision makers. While she is busy getting the job done with excellence, he's leveraging his relationship with the boss. Women believe that they should be recognized for their excellent work and intelligence, capability, and successes but the reality is that they are not boasting about it enough. Women believe the accolades should come naturally and instantly and are disappointed when they do not arrive at all. The man pushes in to this boss's office and celebrates with his boss, which not only brings the win home in the boss's mind but also forms a bond that the female associate may not have. She may not care about bonding in that manner and feels her work should be enough to land her the top job since she's the most qualified. Women, blow your own horn because nobody else is going to do it for you.

There are many other reasons why a woman's salary is less than a man's salary and although those reasons exist I will not elaborate at this time. However, know that it comes from paradigms and beliefs that were created long ago.

Nesting

In my experience as a realtor, I've heard many women express the need to nest. When they are renting a place they cannot make the home the way they want it, perhaps they are unlikely to paint the place because they will have to paint it back to the original colour when they leave or they don't like the kitchen cabinets. The space is not exactly the way she wants it in order to live the lifestyle she craves. For example, she would love to have a home office or a place where she can do her hobby activities and store her stuff. Others want space for people to sleep over when visiting or partying close by. To do that, they feel the need to own the place and be able to invest time and money in arranging the space to suit their needs. Their landlord may not allow work to be done or the tenant may not want to spend money on improving someone else's property. They want to create a space where they can feel vulnerable, safe, calm, and at peace, creative, and they want to host the people they love. We call this nesting. It is a term that is used to refer to women who are in the last few weeks of pregnancy and suddenly have the urge to wash the curtains and scrub the walls and clean things. Lifestyle is important to women who buy their own homes and they plan for their future lives, oftentimes allowing the dream of future children to hold them back from buying what they need now and what they can afford now.

My first bunny, Dutchy, was a gorgeous black tiny dwarf bunny that weighed less than two pounds. She was litter trained and had free rein in the house. She could go anywhere she wanted to and if you closed a door on her she'd rear like a stallion, then kick her back feet and shake her head. Then she would find a way to open the door by pushing it with her head, chewing through it or scratching at it with both paws moving furiously like a boxer on a speed bag. It was quite something to watch. She had her own bedroom and every so often I would notice some strange items in her bedroom closet. I'd find a sock or my husband's tie that had fallen off the hanger, tissues and fluffy stuffing from somewhere (rabbits are notoriously destructive in a house and are constantly chewing so the stuffing could have been from my brand new couch).

One day, I found Maci, my son's very large teddy bear, in her closet. This bear stands 30 inches tall and he had been placed in sitting position on his bedroom floor. Overnight, this tiny bunny pulled the giant Maci all the way out of my son's bedroom and into her bedroom closet. She had started making a nest in his crotch (the teddy bear's crotch, not my son's). It suddenly dawned on me that every month she would build a nest. She was a single bunny and was nowhere near a male bunny so she could not get pregnant but I realized that the behaviour corresponded with my monthly cycle. She was reacting to my pheromones and you could count on it occurring every single month. It was quite something and I tell this story now because the urge to nest is strong.

Once you develop the need to nest nothing will stop you, not even an obstacle that is exponentially larger than you like Maci was for Dutchy. That need to nest is real and is often a driving force behind the desire to purchase a home even for women who are not pregnant.

Instant Cred

Some women believe that property ownership is an opportunity to prove themselves to the world and gain the respect that is automatically given to men. They believe that men get instant cred just by being male and that home ownership and owning investment properties gives women the credibility that they are missing. These women believe they must achieve this goal to prove that they are powerful and to reinforce their power. I believe that the only person you need to please or prove anything to is yourself. However, if the act of buying their own home gives some women the practice they need to become more self-assured I'm all for it. Practise winning and practise success consciousness. It will help you become more confident and more successful.

Sometimes all it takes to gain credibility and to step into your power is to demand it. One day, I had a realtor come to my Seller's house to present an offer to purchase on behalf of his buyers. The Seller had purchased the home on her own and her husband's name was not on title. The four of us sat at the kitchen table where many deals are struck in homes around the country. During a typical offer presentation, the listing agent who represents the Seller maintains control yet allows the other agent to talk about this offer and the client. They may ask a few simple questions of the listing agent for clarity with respect for everyone at the table. The Buyer agents do not ask questions about price, motivation, or other terms and conditions directly to the Seller. The Listing agent must remain in control because the Seller may become uncomfortable should the other agent ask questions that the Seller feels are too personal. Maintaining the power structure serves the Seller and reduces the chance that the Seller may divulge too much information or agree to something without fully understanding the consequences and the obligations they have agreed to.

This realtor did not follow the protocol. He presented the offer directly to my client's husband, joked with him and asked him questions at which point I jumped in and controlled the presentation. I checked my reaction in order to serve my client's best interest, in other words I was firm but I was not so rude that I would inadvertently blow the deal. I directed the conversation back to me in order to regain control of the offer negotiation, however the realtor persisted to ignore me and my client.

I turned to ask my client if she had any questions before I sent the realtor outside to wait and I noticed that her face was beet red. That was proof that she had not only noticed the realtor's actions but was quite upset and insulted by them. I now had the authority to put him in check. I knew she was not pleased with moving forward with this disrespectful man and I wanted to protect her. I walked the realtor out to the front porch and asked him if he wanted to get this deal. He scoffed at me, and told me of course he did, otherwise why would he be here. His attitude was one of disdain and he may have been thinking that I was foolish and unworthy of his attention at this moment. I'm pretty sure he said "dumb question" to himself. I looked him in the eye at close range and told him in order for this deal to move forward to the next step the realtor was going to have to show me and my client the respect we deserved. I asked if he was prepared to do that and he took in a deep breath and agreed. We got the deal done without incident after that.

I retell this story because my client's husband had instant credibility that she and I did not and this was very clearly a bias of gender based on the realtor's belief system. The belief demonstrates the viability of the instant cred that males benefit from and explains why some women feel that they have to earn it through other means and real estate investment fits the bill. You may have experienced this type of scenario yourself in a multitude of ways as most of us do. We are often unaware of it because we've become so accustomed to it that we don't even recognize it for what it is and we often choose to ignore it and allow the status quo. It is a part of our culture and our belief system. Once you recognize it you may take steps to correct the belief.

The future is now

Women buy real estate for their futures. They understand the power of owning property, that it opens up options for whatever lies in their future. There is an old expression, "Life happens when you're busy making plans", which means life will happen and it may not happen how you want it to. The best thing you can do to protect yourself from any unforeseeable circumstance is to give yourself options. Without focusing on the disasters or troubles that you may encounter in life, arm yourself with the tools you may be able to rely on should you ever require them and then go about creating your best life.

One day while multi-tasking I had the TV on in the background and a TV show was playing. This wasn't a show I watched often but the lesson the TV Judge taught that day was brilliant, as I'm sure many were. The Judge caught my attention as she was yelling at a woman because she had allowed herself to be in a position without any options. She had allowed herself to become stuck. She didn't have an education or any marketable skills for working, she didn't have her own money, she didn't even have a credit card, she had no options, and she was backed into a corner. The Judge chastised and told her she should have developed herself and her life differently so that she wouldn't be backed into a corner right now. Then the Judge stopped yelling and lightened up a bit. She explained that it wasn't too late for the woman; she could start now by building a better life for herself that would ensure her freedom to do as she wished.

Owning real estate provides you with options

I had already applied that lesson to my life but had never heard it put so eloquently or loudly and I had never realized that this is what I had done. I asked myself how this information could benefit my clients. It's obvious: owning real estate provides you with options even when life does not happen the way you thought it would. You could sell, rent it out, rent out a portion of the home, you could pull your equity out, or renovate and sell, get partners involved in the business of ownership and so on. Women are arming themselves with a tool box that will allow them choices in the future through property ownership.

As mentioned, men don't require home ownership in order to gain credibility, they possess it through the paradigms of the past that continue to be prevalent today. The men I've worked with who had a budget in mind and soon decide to increase the budget for a home do this without much deliberation. One or two have told me they are comfortable increasing the budget because they know that they'll just earn more money. A woman typically doesn't think that way. They stick to their budget, which is usually under-budgeted and will provide more than ample breathing room and savings for a rainy day. Many times, I've watched women as they have sabotaged their dreams of home ownership for the sake of a few dollars. What a difference in attitude between the male and female home buyer in this scenario. The man is wealth conscious and the woman is poverty conscious.

If he believes he will earn more money he will earn more money. If she believes she won't earn more she probably won't. That's the Law of Attraction. If she rigidly saves for a rainy day and attaches the emotion of worry to the thought the rainy day will surely come. If she limits herself in hopes of protecting herself she will suffer. She will build walls around herself to protect herself and one day those walls will become her jail cell. Live without limits and create options in life and you will see that life will become more beautiful than you can imagine.

Judged on how it looks

When you watch my television shows, *Property Virgins* and *Buy Herself*, you'll notice that women often want the eye candy that men are less concerned with. Women tend to be more concerned about the aesthetic appeal and shy away from properties that are not 100 per cent in line with what they had envisioned for themselves. They may be upset about the style of appliances, the paint colour, and the material of the floor and countertops. It may be because women are judged on how they look and they want their home to look good as well. They also seem to be more sensitive than men are to the opinion of others on how their home looks. They fear being judged based on the eye candy and women are more brand attuned than men and therefore they fear judgement based on those labels. The labels are stainless steel, stone counter, hardwood floor, and brand name toilets. The top priorities are luxuries in the kitchen and bath as those are her sanctuaries. These women are particularly affected by real estate staging and the presentation of the homes for sale. Sellers take note! Prepare your home to show its best and watch the women flock to it.

They feel that they had worked very hard to be able to purchase a home, and they deserve to get everything they want. They've researched the process of home buying, they've read the articles in the media, they've watched the TV shows, they've read the books. Women know what they want, and they want it all. That's awesome and they do deserve it all but sometimes opportunity does not look exactly the way you had planned.

"Confident people make decisions
quickly and firmly."

Many women are information seekers and may experience analysis paralysis if they are not in tune with their goal and have not made the commitment and decision to buy. You'll never be an expert in real estate unless you are in the profession so it would be a good idea to research to a point and then to rely on a network of professionals who will guide you to success with care. Get a bit of info and then act. Don't allow yourself to get sucked into the vortex of information in the media and everyone else's opinions. Build your self-confidence and then make a decision. Confident people make decisions quickly and firmly.

Stay safe

Safety is a top concern for women. They want a safe neighbourhood; they want to feel safe within their condo building. A 24-hour concierge is a desired feature and they are concerned with the level or height of the condo. Many women will not entertain the idea of a condo on the ground floor or 2nd floor and they are concerned about being too high up in case of fire. They are comforted by panic buttons in the gym and parking area, security cameras, and secondary sets of doors in long corridors.

As far as location they tend to want to stay close to family and friends and are willing to take on a longer commute to work if needed. They prefer to live close to where they spend their leisure time.

Contrary to the stereotype that women are incapable of managing their money, these women are very adept at money management. They spend years saving money for a down payment so that their monthly expenses will be lower. It can be true, however, that they become penny wise and pound foolish and miss an opportunity to own a home by to trying to save a few pennies. This can be overcome within the goal-setting exercise explained in this book. It is possible to be fiscally responsible and get what your heart desires.

Owning your own home:
- allows you to heal when you need to and to grow
- gives you a sense of pride and accomplishment that reinforces your self-confidence
- allows you to create a safe space where you can be creative
- allows yourself to dream and to thrive
- provides you with wealth and stability

Owning your own home is the bomb!

CHAPTER 4

Going for a Big Goal Takes Confidence and Knowing Yourself Well

I've worked with many recently separated women who were hoping to buy a home for themselves and their kids. Some of these women come from marriages where they had been living a very nice lifestyle and where money was not a problem. They had grown accustomed to the lifestyle. When these women come to me they often know their expectations are out of whack with what they can afford now that they are on their own and they look to me to help them get aligned with the reality. I willingly help them develop a new mindset, move forward, gain confidence, get clarity, and raise their energy.

I'm rolling more than one woman into this scenario and calling her Rachel. I could see that Rachel was still clinging to her old life and that was a killer! That life was gone. She was facing a whole shift in everything from finances to the emotional side of things. She admitted that she was still hoping she'd get her old life back. I wondered why she would want that if it wasn't so great to begin with, but anyway, she was going to have to make the conscious decision to leave it behind to move ahead.

Confidence makes it possible for you to have a positive attitude

She struggled with having to do it all on her own. She was used to having someone else do it with her or for her. She was afraid of choosing the wrong home, afraid of not having anyone to share the burden, afraid to take responsibility and to be accountable. She was struggling with a lack of confidence. Going for a big goal takes confidence. Confidence makes it possible for you to have a positive attitude and learn what you need to learn to conquer a challenge.

Her self-image had been contested and she had not yet figured out who she was. She was very attached to the labels she had given herself or had been taught about herself – wealthy wife and mother, for example. She was having trouble letting go of the labels and finding out who she was, what she wanted, and how she felt about things. This is no easy task as it requires a total strip down of all the things you think you know about yourself. If you ask yourself, "Who am I?", you may be baffled by the question at first, but with practice the real you starts to come out. For me, it comes out in energy I feel. I can't and don't try to label it. This energy is bigger than any label and cannot be contained in a box. Your mind will be a bad master so don't let your mind answer the question, let the answer come from somewhere else. Give it time, it won't be easy because your mind won't go down without a fight!

I could see that she was going to have to start by breaking down the foundation of everything she knew and start from scratch to build new from there. Call it a teardown or an infill project, like when you want to build a new house. You tear down the whole house that exists and destroy even the foundation. You want to start new to make sure the house you build is on a solid waterproof foundation. You could just add on to the existing house, but you would have to keep the old and try to make it fit with the new. For Rachel, a renovation was not going to cut it. She needed to tear it all down and build new. The old beliefs, the old habits were not going to serve her in her new life. It was time for her to recreate herself with new beliefs and to build her confidence from there. By clinging to the vestiges of her old life she was blocking herself from living in the present and from building a great future. She was desperately trying to keep the old foundation intact but it would have to completely crumble before she could start fresh. I had gone through it. I could see that it was best to let it fall, let it destruct no matter how painful at that time because soon rebuilding would begin and the pain would go away and be replaced with a whole new perspective and entirely new life.

"A closed mind does not allow you to see opportunity nor does it inspire courage."

As we looked at properties, I noticed that she had a tough time envisioning herself in her new life. She was hanging on to the old life and nothing we saw in the way of real estate compared to it. She was blocking herself and too closed to see opportunity. A closed mind does not allow you to see opportunity nor does it inspire courage. She became more picky and negative as we went along and was losing the courage and determination she needed. She was sabotaging herself by being so close-minded.

"When you tap into your true self, you'll find that your true self is love."

Being a good Mom

She was a mom and her kids were the most important thing for her. She wasn't really tapping into what she wanted as a person; she was thinking too much as a mother. She was aligned with her role as mother but had allowed herself to lose contact with her inner desires in doing so. She could better help them adjust by making a decision that made her feel good about herself and her life and thus become a good influence on them. Obviously, you aren't going to get a one bedroom and say "Forget the kids!" but by not tapping in to what she wanted and needed and by not keeping an open mind she was hurting everyone. Being a good mom is not all about sacrifice. It can be about displaying a sense of self, confidence, and empowerment. When you tap into your true self, you'll find that your true self is love. Being a good mom is not about being a good cook or being the cupcake decorator. It's about leading by example, being yourself, allowing others to be themselves, and loving them and loving yourself.

Rachel didn't buy a home right away because she still needed more time and effort to get into the right head space; she needed to do more work on herself. I know she would have benefitted from more positive self-talk and from activities that would build her confidence. By encouraging herself to dream about what she wanted, by writing it down and repeating it to herself she would have developed the self-confidence she needed.

Even though she could not make the decision to buy a home at that precise time, by doing some work on herself she would have changed her self-image. She needed encouragement to remove self-doubt and she would be able to gain the encouragement from her self-talk. The opposite is true as well as she might have told herself she couldn't and she would have proven herself right. She was allowing her past to be too big a factor in her perception. Until she let the past go she would be pulled back every time.

Choose your thoughts carefully, become aware of your self-image and of the things you tell yourself. Do they serve you well? They are just stories you tell yourself so choose the stories that will help you get what you want. Stop choosing and creating the stories that work against you and opt for the ones that help you achieve your dreams.

We believe what we're taught

I was raised to be a wife and mother. Be a good wife and a good mother and you will be successful. The man is smarter, he makes the money, he is strong and knows everything. I actually believed that stuff. Don't judge me. If I had been taught that the world was flat I would have believed that too. I mean, how was I to know that it wasn't true?

When I married, I believed the man was stronger, smarter, the bread winner. Gradually, I began to realize that it wasn't so. I was smart, I was strong, and I was the bread winner.

I could figure things out, I'm a problem solver. I could handle pressure, I was resourceful and could resolve issues, I would roll up my sleeves and get it done. I was strong, I could take whatever life threw at me. And, as it turned out, I liked having more than one job, or working 60 hours or more a week. I had gumption, I was brave, I had initiative. I wasn't going to sit around moaning, I was going to do something about it, whatever it was.

When I was a kid my parents were quite well off and money was no issue. One day I asked my dad for $25 for a pair of jeans: Levi's, they were the 'in' thing. I was in Grade 9 and had grown over the summer so my jeans were very tight; I had outgrown them. In those days, we used to lie on the bed and use a wire hanger to pull the zipper up, that's how tight we wore our jeans. For me to want a bigger pair of jeans, they must have been really uncomfortable! I asked very politely for the money. My dad leaned over, pulled out his wallet and pulled out a fiver. He handed it to me. I looked at it, and thought, "Oh hell, now what?" You see, in our house you showed respect always, so I wasn't going to dis him, but I had to get more money.

I said, "Oh. I said twenty-five dollars, not five dollars. Levi's are twenty-five dollars" very respectfully. He replied, "I heard you, but if you can't find a pair of jeans for five dollars, then you don't need them badly enough." Which was laughable because of my camel toe, it seemed pretty obvious just how badly I needed the jeans. So, I did what every kid did when one parent didn't give the right answer, I went to the other. Now, understand, my parents had the money. My mom walked into a jeweller one day and bought herself a three-carat diamond ring. It cost a hell of a lot more than a pair of Levi's. So, I went to my mom and said, "Daddy won't give me twenty-five dollars" and told her the story. She said, "He's right." So off I went to the low end mall and discovered that even there five bucks wasn't enough, so I had to go the children's store and find a pair of jeans on sale.

The five buck lesson

The point of the story is that some people were never given the opportunity to learn the value of a dollar as a kid and grew up without an appreciate or understanding of how to get it or why they should. My dad provided everything we needed and then some but also taught us that it was his money that he had earned for work he had done, for smarts he had used and if I wanted to buy anything I wanted I was going to have to understand the value of money and make my own. My dad taught me another valuable lesson that day. I didn't enjoy having to rely on someone else to give me what I wanted. I learned that if I didn't want to rely on someone else for money I should earn my own money, which, by the way, went against the paradigm of becoming a wife and mother and relying on a husband for everything.

In my twenties, I had a big mortgage, with a 13.75 percent interest rate, and I had to go on a business trip. I gave my partner the money to pay the mortgage, around $2,200. We had no extra cash back then. Times were tough. He was starting a new career and wasn't making much money yet so I was working extra jobs to make ends meet. I didn't mind, I liked working, and I knew it wouldn't be forever. I handed over the cash, told him what it was for, and went on my business trip. This is how I recall the following events. He picked me up at the airport and on the way home I asked, just to make conversation I guess, if he had paid the mortgage. I shouldn't have to ask a 28-year-old man if he had paid the bills as we had discussed, but I did. He replied, "No, I didn't," and I thought he was joking. I asked again, because I didn't want to believe it.

This was 1991, Canada was in a recession and money was tight. Trying to keep calm I asked what he had spent it on. He said he didn't know. I started to lose it. I mean, did he buy a couch or something? No, it seems that he went out partying with the guys. I couldn't breathe. I couldn't understand how anyone could do that. He knew how hard I worked for that money, and he knew there wasn't any more money. He knew the mortgage had to be paid, and yet he had gone to bars blowing the money I had given him to pay the mortgage. I couldn't believe it. I was scared. What now? Are we going lose the house? I don't want to lose the house. What would happen if we lost the house? I'd be home-less. I'd be shattered. I worked hard, I had the money, I gave it to my partner to pay the mortgage. I didn't know what happened to people who didn't pay the mortgage, but I knew it wasn't good. I was afraid of banks, I was afraid of mortgage companies. I knew I couldn't just say, "My partner blew the money on booze and bitches, playing the big shot with the money I slaved at two jobs to get, please forgive us."

I balled up in the second bedroom of our unpaid-for home, sobbing wracking sobs, scared, disbelieving, feeling betrayed, knowing he didn't give me a second thought while he had gone out and partied with my hard-earned cash that had been destined for the credit union. How does this happen? He's not a foolish teenager without respect or a care in the world. He was a grown man! I was crying so hard I could barely get breaths of air in. I was so upset about being deceived, about being broke, about being in arrears, about envisioning him blowing the money I made on other women, on booze and who knows what else. This may not sound like a big deal to you, but remember, I was taught to believe the man is smarter, financially responsible, reliable, trustworthy, and would take care of me. My head was spinning. I came really close to a breakdown. How much more could I take? How much more of a good partner could I be? What had I done wrong, to deserve this? My paradigm caused me to believe that it was my fault of course.

I'm *just* a woman?

But suddenly a glimmer of lucidity triggered a radical thought: could all of that information they fed me be false? Could I be the financially responsible one in this relationship? What did I know about money . . . nothing other than how hard it seemed to make it and how fast it could disappear. Could I be, wait don't say it, the smarter one? What? How can that be? I'm just a woman.

Thirty years later, it seems impossible that I could be that ill-informed, so insecure and unsure of my capabilities. Or does it? I had been cling-ing to my conditioned beliefs. I know how I became that way, and I know I had to go through something earth-shattering like discovering that men are not smarter, stronger, financially savvy as a rule before I would allow myself to act. My whole life had been built on that faulty foundation, and it was just a matter of time before it came crumbling down and crumble it did. The belief had to be destroyed for me to realize my true potential.

"The belief had to be *destroyed* for
me to realize my true potential."

The very foundation of my belief system had to be *destroyed* so that I could rise up, dust myself off (although the residue lingered for decades and had gotten into the fabric of my being) and realize that I could achieve, I could do things, I could be things that I never ever dreamed I could.

How the hell does this happen in modern times to a woman who had achieved academic success and accolades in the workplace? It started at birth, if not before.

Imagine Susan Boyle, the singer from *Britain's Got Talent* who blew the minds of the world when she sang, *I Have a Dream.* I once read somewhere that she was told that she had suffered brain damage during her birth. Imagine, thinking your whole life that you have brain damage. It turns out, it was a misdiagnosis and she has a higher than average IQ but has Asperger's. Imagine how limiting her dreams were and how the people around her treated her, what their expectations of her were and in turn, what her own expectations became.

I feel like I was told I was not capable because I was a woman due to a weird culture within my family. It is the same kind of stigma that made me not even want to try. I was an honour student but once I saw for myself that I could get nineties, I never wanted/dared to get good grades. I thought it would challenge everything I was taught and believed about myself. Maybe deep down I also thought that I would not be attractive to a man if I were too smart, but I think it was more likely that I never thought I would be smart enough for it to be a problem.

Be a secretary and marry your boss? No!

How does that even happen? I lived in a house where I was told I was only good enough to be wife and mother, was laughed at when I said I wanted to go to law school. Outside of the family, my intellectual capabilities were celebrated. I was on the honours list, I was in the test group of smart kids who got to do split classes, who got to audition for band class. Kids knew me as a smart kid. Why then, did I accept a less worthy version of myself? Because it was easier to believe that. Because I didn't want to cause problems for myself or the people around me. What a fool I was!

Further, when I went to work I was a rock star. I was very capable, valued as an employee, and I loved working. Then I would go home and accept the fact that I should strive to be a secretary so I could marry my boss. Why didn't I cling to the more respected version of me, why did I cling to the lower opinion? Simply because I believed my own story, the one I created in my head and found support for at home. At home there was support for the higher vision of myself but I was blind to it, I was not open to see it. I chose to cling to the negative perception of me.

I wish I had gone to a school counsellor who would tell me I could do anything I wanted to, and that I should start dreaming about careers, start researching about the world and what jobs were out there already. I only saw women working as teachers and secretaries, as bank tellers and in hair salons. There is only a slight chance that it would have made a difference for me anyway. My mind was made up.

I slowly started to realize that I was going to have to take care of myself. That marriage was critical to my progression as an independent woman and I am very grateful for it. I knew I had to rely on myself. The world I knew collapsed around me as I came to realize that everything I had learned was bullshit.

How selfish!

I remember telling someone that the relationship was over and she responded, "But don't you want to have kids?" which shocked me. I mean, I was young, 29 years old, I had time. I could find happiness with a man and time to have a child. And, did she really think I should stay in the marriage just to have a kid? She said it was selfish to not want to have a child. Selfish? So, saving myself from a lifetime of unhappiness, where either I'd destroy my ex or he'd destroy me was selfish? Or did she mean that not wanting a child was selfish? I didn't ask. I was too shocked to dwell on it. I didn't want the answer really. I had made up my mind and for once I was going to do what I knew was best for me. How selfish.

I had put my happiness on a list of things I deserved. Holy cow, that didn't go over well with the people around me and they struggled with my new beliefs. I put self-respect on a list of things I deserved as well as respect from my spouse. I shook off the heavy burden of always doing what everyone else wanted me to do. It was like a heavy, black wool full length cape with a hood over my head and partially covering my eyes. It came off, and I felt like I could fly. I would learn over and over again that many of the fibres of that heavy black cape had clung to me and would try to knit together with the other fibres to cloak me in the darkness once again. It stuck to me, the feeling that I was not as capable as men or many other women or smart enough or pretty enough or anything good enough and it would try my confidence over and over and over.

Transition doesn't come easily

I worked with Danielle as she was transitioning from a married woman to a divorcée. It was time to move on and move forward. Buying a home on her own became challenging as she struggled to determine exactly what it was she wanted. She had grown attached to the mindset of always thinking about what would make someone else happy and had never been able to focus completely on what her dreams and desires were. She felt that she had always chosen to sacrifice her own desires to make the other person happy.

Changing this habit does not come naturally for many women. Danielle could focus on herself and yet she was trapped in language that did not serve her well. Her thoughts were that she would make her own decisions but then she'd have to suffer from poor choices. She believed she was not able to make good decisions and the words she used expressed this belief. Empowerment would alter the language to, "These choices will be mine alone, and I will reap the rewards." To get her to think in the new way would require a change in her mindset and demonstrate her ability to make sound decisions.

Danielle believed that thinking of herself and for herself was something negative and not a benefit of being human. It was something she felt she would be forced to do and not a basic right. I wanted her to think "I am embracing the opportunity to decide what I truly want." She made it sound like it was a chore, an obstacle or something negative that she had to endure. With new language she would be more likely to change her mind and achieve the desired results.

She felt she had sacrificed for love, and I asked her to open her eyes to see that she now could really choose for love of herself. She was taking a big step toward her new life, her real self and her happiness. Many women cling to a piece of furniture or other object from their previous life when they were part of a couple. They often miss out on wonderful properties that are too small to comfortable hold the massive desk, bed or armoire and Danielle was no different. We had to work on letting go of old relics of the past, including habits that did not serve her well. I had to keep her focused on the moment at hand.

It was especially difficult because we were touring homes in an area that was attractive to young families. Every child's toy or playroom triggered a response from my client as she would find herself mourning the dream of a family of her own. I needed to get her out of those neighbourhoods and get her into areas that had a more varied demographic where she would not be reminded daily that she did not have a child.

The process of looking for a home actually helped her determine her desires, which in turn helped her to heal and to create the new version of herself. She had to dig deep to search for the true wish list that was strictly hers and that would give her a sense of home with her new understanding of herself. She was able to shirk the old life and embrace the new one that served her well at that moment.

She made a compromise by giving up some of the things on her wish list so that she could be closer to friends, which made her more socially connected, which made her happier. She had redefined herself by tapping in to her true self and creating her new reality. She was excited to begin a new journey her way.

Stepping outside the comfort zone

Chloe had never lived on her own and had not yet decided how to envision her new home. The type of home she bought would depend on her decision to have her own space versus having tenants live in her home. Your list of fears and priorities will dictate what kind of property you buy. Understand that the fears are the reasons why you behave a certain way and the priorities are the symptoms of the fears.

Chloe was unable to make a decision until she had come to understand her true motivation. Her motivation was not to pay down the mortgage faster, instead it was to live in a nice comfortable home with aesthetic appeal. It took some time for her to understand herself but as soon as she did she was able to find the right property and even the fact that she was in multiple offers did not stop her. She had made a decision and had become driven and bought the home.

"To set a goal from a negative does not serve you well so change it from a reaction of fear of being judged to acknowledging that you have the desire to achieve this goal."

Set a healthy goal

Christina was at the stage of life when all of her friends were getting married and buying homes and she felt they would judge her for being different. This is not a healthy way to set a goal so I like to change it to a more positive version by saying that she saw her friends doing it and thought that she could and should do it as well. To set a goal from a negative does not serve you well so change it from a reaction of fear of being judged to acknowledging that you have the desire to achieve this goal and accept that you can do it. Her friends had made the move to build their future wealth and security and she could too.

Safety is a prime concern for many women when buying their own homes. She had grown comfortable with having a roommate around and was very concerned about safety as she was going to be living on her own for the first time. While aesthetics and space were important to her she understood that the main thing she would not give up on was safety. She needed to feel safe and that meant that certain neighbour-hoods and buildings were off her list. We were able to find a beautiful yet small place that gave her a sense of pride of ownership and allowed her to feel completely safe.

These women experienced their own issues with determining what it was they wanted and as soon as they were able to tap into an under-standing of themselves they were able to make a decision they were happy with very quickly.

Why do you want to own a home?

This may seem like an easy question to answer. But, it varies from person to person. You may feel it's the next step, the natural progression of your life. For some, it's being able to feel like you've made it. For others, it allows you to plant roots and gives your life stability. And for others it represents a vehicle to financial freedom. There are so many reasons for people to buy real estate. What's yours?

What does home ownership mean to you? Name all the things. Really! Do this, right now. Make a list of what it would mean to you to own real property. Take your time, think long about this. It could be a long list, or it could be a list with just one item on it. Be honest with yourself and think about what drives you to own real estate.

After you've completed the exercise look at the list you created, and notice which ones make you get out of bed and turn on the laptop or check out the mobile app to look up properties for sale. Which ones make you talk or dream of real estate all the time? Which ones are really important to you?

Put that list away for 2–5 days. Retrieve it and review it. Do all of those things you wrote on the list still hold true? Are there more to add or some to remove? Give it some more thought, and again, be honest with yourself. If it's to keep up with the Jones's then write it down. No judgment here, don't stop yourself from listing something just because you think it's bad, or others would scorn you. Really dig deep and pull out the most important reasons why you want to buy a place. It may take some time to complete this first part of the exercise, so don't worry if you need to leave it and come back to it a few times before you are satisfied that it has been nailed down.

Don't read this part until you've completed the exercise above.

Once you have your list, make space for a full paragraph underneath each and every item. I want you to elaborate on your list and to be specific about why that item appears on your list. Don't just write, "Because I don't want to pay rent." Make a whole paragraph explaining why paying rent for the rest of your life doesn't agree with your life plans. Get as detailed as you can, for example, "if I rent at $2,000 per month and spend $24,000 on rent in one year I will lose that $24,000 forever, and I will have lost the opportunity to build equity through home ownership for another year."

That's good – but keep going, dig deeper, get passionate about it.

"I don't want to pay someone else's mortgage because I want to pay down my own mortgage, because I begrudge my landlord's success. He's mean and doesn't help his tenants so I don't want him to prosper off of me. I despise when someone prospers off of me because I feel like they don't deserve it. I deserve to prosper off of my own actions, nobody else does! Why should he get rich and not me? Why should I help him get rich instead of helping myself get rich?! No way! I'm going to make myself rich by paying my own mortgage off. Yeah. baby!"

That's more like it! Can you go deeper?

"I don't want to be like my (fill in the blank with Dad, friend, sister, aunt) who didn't buy a house until she was 45 years old and had to pay a mortgage until she was 70 years old and missed out on a huge amount of profit. Or worse, I don't want to be like (fill in the blank) who never ended up buying a place and rented or lived with her parents until they died. I want to be able to pay off my mortgage quickly so I can have spare money to travel, to open a business, to do whatever I want to do. I don't want to be in a position where the landlord can raise my rent and still not fix the broken thing, or the leaky tap, or to be able to sell the place and kick me out before I am ready to go."

Yeah, that's good. Feel it. Keep writing. Every time you write something, ask yourself why, like a little four-year-old. They never stop asking why. They ask why the sky is blue, you answer with whatever you recall from your school days or the program *Nova*. They ask again, "But why?" and this goes on and on. Go for it, ask why again and again until you've gone so deep that you might even have surprised yourself. Once you feel you have exhausted all of the reasons why that item is important to you move on down the list and do it, really well for each and every item on the list. Warning, you may become very excited!

Your reason for wanting to buy a home may be that you feel the need to nest. Ask yourself what that really means to you. Perhaps that it would allow you to get a rescue dog. You are having a problem finding a landlord that will accept a dog, and you don't want to live without a dog because there are so many abused or abandoned dogs that need your help and you want to add that amazing love to your life. You want a secure back yard to let him be outside a lot, and you want to be able to walk or run at night and feel safe with a big dog. You miss your family dog so much and you just can't handle living without that companionship any longer. Why? Because having a dog makes me feel loved. Why? Because dogs give unconditional love. Why do you want that? Because life can be hard, and sometimes I feel lonely, like nobody really understands me. Why? Because I don't fit the mold. Why? Because I am not like them, because I am more creative, or less so. Keep going. Keep asking WHY.

See how deep you can go

This level of introspection, self-reflection, looking deep into your true self will help you in all aspects of your life. You may experience an A-HA moment where something you had previously never allowed your conscious mind to accept about yourself has been allowed to appear. You have shone light on it, acknowledged it, written it down, and now you can release it. You don't have to dwell on it and you don't have to own it, just allow it to be.

Now that you're done with this step, take a look at which items on your list of reasons why you want to buy real estate you had very little to say about. Most likely, those were just superficial reasons and perhaps they were reasons other people told you that you should care about but those reasons never really resonated with you. Those ones should go to the bottom of your list, but they can stay on the list. They may come into play later on. Before you move them to the bottom, make certain that you have asked WHY enough times for you to truly determine the underlying reason for having it on your list. It may be that you are blocking yourself from understanding a part of yourself.

"Focus on what you want and avoid writing your goal in language that gives priority to what you *don't* want."

Now you must turn any negative thought into a positive. If you thought, "I don't want to pay someone else's mortgage for them by renting" change it to the positive version. "I will build my own wealth through property ownership." Write "I want to give a deserving dog a safe and loving home." You may write, "I want to buy real estate just because I want to." Focus on what you want and avoid writing your goal in language that gives priority to what you don't want.

I hope this exercise has given you a clear understanding of what is important to you when you dream about owning real estate. This list should be kept in a safe place, one where you can easily access it whenever you want. Guard it well, be certain not to lose it and don't take it for granted. If you followed the above suggestions you have something very powerful and we will revisit it often.

This list is important for those who are buying their first homes as well as those who are planning to buy investments properties, and those planning to downsize or upsize. This list will help keep you on the right track when things start to go off the rails. Rarely does a real estate purchase go exactly as planned or happen as easily as just walking into an open house and buying it. It can happen all nice and easy that way, but in my experience in a very expensive city like Toronto the process of buying a house isn't for sissies. There will be some serious hurdles to overcome before you will become successful. If you don't want it badly enough you won't do it. This list will remind you why you started doing this in the first place and will pick you up after a debilitating loss in multiple offers when you were sure you had nailed it. It will strengthen you, encourage you, excite you, and motivate you. It will be your guiding beacon. Cherish it, it's part of you and will help you achieve your real estate dream.

CHAPTER 5

Rich People Play to Win,
Poor People Play NOT to Lose

My friend Marcella came from a single mom upbringing. There was not a lot of money and often not enough. She grew up in an area where it was accepted to be brought up by a single parent and there was no stigma attached to it. Her mom is her hero, the most incredible person she has ever met in her life. Mom would often tell her that she was loved, she was amazing, she had real potential. All these good things, and you might expect that Marcella was going to be well adjusted and driven to achieve her potential. The truth is, she saw a disconnect between what her mom was telling her and what her mom truly believed about herself, which led Marcella to believe her mom wasn't telling her the truth and therefore did not believe the beautiful empowering words.

Regardless of the message her mom was trying to instill in her Marcella beat herself up a lot and it reverberated into the way she thinks about herself. She, like me and many others, believes that self-deprecation is funny but it is a dangerous habit and we have to stop doing it.

One night out, Marcella found a beautiful guy who seemed to be standing there waiting for her to approach him so she went to speak to him. She could not believe that he was interested in her because she felt she didn't deserve someone as good looking as him. She gained confidence in his vulnerability. He was a new immigrant, did not speak a lot of English, and was feeling rather lonely and uncertain in his new country. Marcella was still so intimidated by him. He was so good looking, perfect almost, and she felt ugly because of the long-standing beliefs she had created in her mind. She says that she had that one glimmer of belief that she was deserving and then it was gone again, replaced by doubt she built up over the years.

The marriage broke down, Marcella became very unhappy, and this manifested in weight gain and anger. She took steps to end the marriage by acting out in an irrational manner. She didn't just sit him down and let him know that it was time to move on, to seek true happiness in love. Instead, she created a situation where she made a huge problem out of something that was totally manufactured in her mind, and all of her pent-up frustration and disappointment came out in the form of rage. It ended the marriage abruptly, and she takes full responsibility for the incident.

She acted that way because she felt she needed an excuse to leave a guy everyone loved and to end a marriage just because you weren't happy wasn't really good enough reason. That was her paradigm and it was mine in my first marriage as well.

Your success may look like someone else's failure

Most people don't applaud you when you do something solely for the purpose of happiness. My friends Rick and Sabina had saved money, purchased their first home, saved more money, and bought an investment property in Newfoundland with a plan. The plan was that they would sell the condo and live in the RV for three years so they could retire young, and travel around Canada in their RV until they were ready to settle down in Newfoundland in the place they had bought and rented out to tenants. Once settled, they would find new jobs and start a family. It took a lot of planning and sacrifice but they were committed. The two of them lived in the RV with very little living space through hot summers and cold winters. It was difficult at times but they kept their eyes on the goal and soon they were able to serve notice at work.

Can you guess at how people at work reacted to the news of 40-year-old Rick's early retirement? Not one of them expressed any happiness for him. As a matter of fact, they were angry with him and many people stopped talking to him altogether. Is that what you had imagined or did you imagine a celebration, a retirement party, slaps on the back, atta' boy and joyous laughter?

Here's why they reacted that way. Simply, his success at reaching his far-fetched goal made them each feel bad about their own lives, about what they perceived to be their failure. They perceived him to be superior and themselves inferior. It's possible they had previously believed they were superior and Rick's success challenged those feelings of superiority.

In the movie *My Big Fat Greek Wedding 2*, the father, you know the guy with the Windex said something very deep. He said, "When you are successful you become the sign of hope of the optimist but to the pessimist you represent the stink of his own failure."

For Rick's co-workers, his success had become the stink of their own failure. The failure to set a goal and achieve it. Failure to work towards a better life, toward their happiness, a sense of fulfillment, to allow joy in their lives. They reacted to the fact that they had not allowed themselves to dream freely. Not all of them would have the dream to RV across Canada, and then move to Newfoundland but based on their reaction, all of them at some point had wished for more for themselves and had failed to get it. Rick and Sabina's success shone a bright light on those failures, on the unhappiness and the feeling of being stuck.

"With a strong desire to be free it will be so."

Everyone has a choice and consciousness is recognizing that you always have choice. You may allow yourselves to think that a person, a job or a situation has left you without a choice but the truth is very different. You have allowed yourselves to be placed in a proverbial jail cell and you refuse to acknowledge that the door is wide open. With a strong desire to be free it will be so. Instead, you allow your fears and limiting beliefs to overpower the desire for freedom and to keep you there in that jail cell. As Marianne Williamson said, "it's our light not our darkness that most frightens us."

Being yourself is something nobody can take away from you

I had been divorced, experienced financial ruin, and I was ready to reshape myself. At the age of 31, I asked myself, "What do I want to be when I grow up?" I was ready for change and somewhere deep inside I believed that I was worthy of more, that I deserved more and I that should have more. I decided I wanted to pursue a career in law and I studied and took the LSAT. I scored above average and applied as a mature student to the law schools in Canada.

I remember that when I told some people of my plan they laughed but I didn't let that stop me. When I told one person of my plan she asked, "Don't you ever want to have children?" She was a stay-at-home-mom by choice. She and her husband had discussed how they would like to raise their children based on their beliefs and put it into motion. I replied, "I'm not having a hysterectomy, I'm just applying to law school. I want to be a lawyer, I am pursuing a career in law." Her explanation for her comment was that she believed that staying at home with her kids would ensure that they would grow up to be well-adjusted law-abiding people and would not be out committing drive-by shootings.

My snarky retort was that I was pretty sure that Sandra Day O'Connor's kids were not committing drive-by shootings and that a woman could have a successful career and still be a mom. I probably used the term "good mom", that a woman could be a Supreme Court Judge and still be a good mother. I wouldn't use the words "good mother" these days because it seems to indicate that woman should strive to adhere to societal norms in order to achieve a judgment that is flawed.

'Enter Super Mom!

That label has caused a lot of anxiety and stress for women. That's why we see the rise of the legend of Super Mom. The woman who has it all: the career, money, family, the perfect kids, she is the perfect daughter, wife, sister, daughter-in-law and feeds the family and the poor with homemade food that she grows on the homestead. She saves all the stray animals, heals the environment and still has time to play a perfect game of golf. It's impossible to achieve Super Mom status for so many reasons including the fact that someone else is judging you on whatever criteria they choose and the criteria may fluctuate. As soon as you get good at golf the game changes to yoga.

We feel that we will not be worthy of the love of our family unless we do this, that our children will be ridiculed if our cupcakes are made from a box and not from scratch. Has my self-worth come down to a cupcake recipe? Am I less of a person for not baking them from scratch? Think about how ridiculous that is. But I'll bet there are tons of us who have felt this way and have succumbed to the pressure and have found ourselves baking late at night, foregoing the activity I really wanted to do or the work my client needed done just so that our kids would fit in by bringing homemade cupcakes.

It may seem like I am making fun of the woman who told me I couldn't be a lawyer and a mother but I'm not. I know that her beliefs and her life are her own and that they differ from mine. We have taken on our various beliefs about ourselves and about life. Her words did nothing to stop me, I continued to aspire toward a career in law, however it never happened for me and I don't regret it. I've learned a lot and I will never have to regret not trying. It led me to where I am today. I found my niche and I am so happy that I can afford to celebrate others who are happy, who find their path to achieving their purpose. It's a good place to be.

I continue to become more and more self-aware each day. I take steps to improve by overcoming obstacles that are the limiting beliefs that do not serve me. I may deal with my own paradigms every day for the rest of my life or I may find a way to be completely free of them forever. Either way, I'm committed to living as my true self. I know one thing, being yourself is something that nobody can take away from you unless you let them.

My friend Marcella was able to reach a point in her awareness where she could actually not give a darn about what anyone thought. She could release people in her life who did not serve her well, whose beliefs did not support her. She could eliminate people from her life who were not giving her what she needed. She had defined her core values and lived by them. She decided to surround herself with people who would honour those values and she let the rest of the people go.

Surround yourself with the energy that serves you

Not everyone will like or accept your goals and desires; they may try to keep you down. Your obligation to yourself is to surround yourself with the energy that serves you and not to shrink yourself because of what someone else will think. What someone else thinks of you is none of your business. Remembering this will help you remain true to yourself once you have become aware of yourself. You need to recommit to your goal and connect with your WHY many times, using auto suggestion in order to develop the persistence to be able to overcome the paradigms of others.

Sometimes their paradigms will settle in with your new energy and other times they will be vehemently upset and will not be able to cope. It may sound cold-hearted (if it does it's your paradigm speaking), but you must choose yourself over anyone else, especially the people who try to keep you down. You may need to let them go. This should not be taken lightly and I am not suggesting that you should just abandon family and friends callously. Once you know yourself well you will be able to analyze your relationships and determine which, if any, hold you back from expressing your true self.

The 40-year-old clean up

I didn't realize that I was doing this very thing but at around 40 years old I started cleaning house. I guess you could say that I'd been to the puppet show and had seen the strings. If someone wasn't feeding my soul they were gone. The people who drained my energy and never fed my soul, and the people who made me feel bad about myself were gone. I cleaned up. I realized that I deserved to be respected for my true self and if this didn't resonate with them they were cut off. I'm in an industry that requires a lot of energy and working with people can drain your energy at times. I wasn't going to spend my precious free time with people I dreaded being with. I had to be ruthless with my time. If they didn't support my goals and my core values they were gone. It was a step into freedom and I'm proud of myself for taking it.

You may find that the only thing holding you back is your own paradigm. You may be imagining that they won't accept you if you change so you resist change. Oftentimes, the change is welcomed and it benefits everyone around you. You may be afraid to be lonely but if you are not able to be yourself it is better to be alone. I learned this first hand during my first marriage. I had been very lonely in that marriage and being alone was no match for that kind of loneliness. Being lonely in a relationship is much worse than being alone. I know, I've been in both of those scenarios. I had to be in a new relationship with myself, introspecting, growing, creating, thriving, finding myself for real.

"Become aware of the limiting beliefs
you've previously accepted as truth."

Marcella felt that it was liberating to be able to let go of caring what they thought even for a brief moment. Many of us would have to keep on top of this and work on maintaining the level of confidence and self-love to be able to stay in that mindset because the old paradigms will want to run things again. Insecurity, anxiety and self-deprecation may reappear over and over again. If you wish to develop the self-confidence to live the life you choose to live you must become aware of the limiting beliefs you've previously accepted as truth and change them to the beliefs that will allow you to dream and achieve. The best way to do this is through repetition and keeping those new beliefs top of mind.

Thoughts are either supportive or non-supportive and although we cannot control the thought that comes into our mind we can choose how we will deal with it. Don't own the thought, let it go. If you wish to try an exercise simply be aware of the thought that does not serve you and replace it with the opposite. Write it out if you wish, then put a big X through it, and then rip it up. Then write the supportive thought out making sure it is the opposite of the thought you had. You must learn how to control your thoughts or they will continue to control you. If this type of non-supportive thought has been with you for a long time it may be particularly stubborn and you will have to consistently replace it with the polar opposite belief, repeating the new belief regularly and with persistence. It may keep popping up with language that it knows will trigger you. It's sneaky and devilish so be on the lookout today, tomorrow and always.

> "You must learn how to control your thoughts
> or they will continue to control you."

Marcella has grown since her divorce and has become more confident. She mentions that when she was younger, even after her divorce, she would not allow herself to dream, to set a challenging goal. She wasn't ready to experience failure and was afraid to try to strive for more. She felt it would crush her and be too difficult to overcome if she tried and failed. "I wouldn't be able to get up the next day, that would have broken me." She knew it was easier and safer to just stay the way she was. To Marcella, at that moment in her life, keeping the status quo seemed to be the appropriate method of self-help. She recognizes now that this was a sad way to exist and is grateful she recognized that something had to change and then acted on it.

Living without goals can lead to depression and a feeling of being lost. I felt that way in 2016–2018. Once I realized I had somehow stopped goal-setting I immediately took steps to rectify it and made the choice to dream about the life I wanted to create for myself. The book *Think and Grow Rich* by Napoleon Hill helped me as did *The Science of Getting Rich* by Wallace D. Wattles and so many other books. I became more energized, optimistic and could appreciate what I had with more gratitude. If you're feeling lost and without hope, start reading those books and see what an enormous change will come about in your attitude and in your life.

In Marcella's mind, her marriage breakdown represented a cause for more disappointment for her mom. Her mother had really loved her son-in-law and although she had been very disappointed in the break-up, she never chastised her daughter. Yet Marcella felt she had let her mother down and wasn't ready to risk letting her down again. Her mother was heartbroken over the break-up but always supported her daughter's happiness. Women often worry themselves with the business of making everyone else happy, which can often cause them to forfeit their dreams for the sake of someone else's happiness. Those actions can cause anxiety, depression and loss of a sense of self.

Marcella manufactured the belief that her mom had been disappointed in her and thus Marcella resented her own failure and could not see that it was a win. Marcella had had the courage it took to change a situation that had been holding her back. Even though she had been unaware of what she had been doing she had changed the external circumstances in order to begin working on the internal ones. Perhaps the opposite is true, she changed her internal circumstances and then worked on the external ones.

Marcella said, "I'm no Rosa Parks but I am my own person who is still trying every day to be better. I want to be better in all capacities of my life. Ten years ago I didn't care about that, I didn't care about being better. Something has changed. I want the greatness but I also want to give back, be humble, be loving and all of those things that I scoffed at 10 years ago. I scoffed at introspection, getting to know myself better, meditation, it just didn't resonate with me at that time." I asked if she had been afraid to envision her own greatness and her reply was that she had been afraid to see herself at all.

We had been working together for a few years and Marcella decided to create a vision board. She gives me credit for inspiring this action. She remembers that I had asked her and the other associates if anyone was going to be financially secure when they retired. I said, "They say you need to have $2.5 million to retire when you're 65. Will you? Nobody is saving enough these days and the sad reality is that their future may be bleak. Owning property is the road to financial freedom." I don't recall the incident but those are words I often say, so I wholeheartedly take credit for it!

Marcella created a vision board with an income goal, a trip to the Amalfi Coast of Italy, and a two-bedroom condo. When I was filming *Property Virgins* I showed the same style of suite in the very building Marcella later bought in. She said when she had seen it on the show she had set in her mind that it was exactly what she wanted. Marcella says that she watched as many people, including single women like her, buy great properties on my show. She mentioned that watching all of these people do it gave her the courage to do it, and she set a goal.

A few years later, while she had been working out of the country, she shared her plans to purchase and asked for my help. We set up a plan so that her mom could come to town for a few days of solid home touring so she could get a good idea of what was happening in the market. The style of unit she had loved years earlier became available. It was not a two bedroom but it was a one bedroom plus a den that was as large as many bedrooms. It seemed perfect for her! The problem was that the Seller had set an unreasonable asking price and I had taken issue with that. My friend was waiting for me to give her that extra little push into the deal even though it would mean that she would have to pay $14,000 too much for the suite. She was waiting for me to cheer her on and support her. I was struggling, I was in protector mode and giving off the wrong vibes. My attitude and my energy confused her. I was teaching her to be afraid and I almost sabotaged her! My own paradigm was getting in the way of her success.

My husband is my business partner and he had come along for this as he really loved my friend and her mom. He got on the phone to her and told her not to rob herself of the dream of home ownership for the sake of $14,000. She says that his words gave her to nudge she needed and she went ahead and took the deal. After the fact, I was happy and relieved that she had bought it but during the offer negotiations I had been a detriment to my own friend. I'm so glad that my husband had been the voice of reason and that she made the purchase. She's made so much money on that property and I am very proud of her. She even went to the Amalfi Coast. This stuff works whether you believe it or not!

I asked her what home ownership has done for her.

"I am proud. My pride comes from having the type of home everyone wants to visit. I wanted a place where my mom was proud of being there, she could have her own room, she could stay with me when she ages. That pride of having the place where it's nice, the amenities are beautiful, the area is familiar to me it's comfortable, nostalgic, I truly did buy my first forever home. It was the most emotional thing that I had ever felt, not even getting married was as emotional as that. It was so unbelievably satisfying that at that moment I felt that I could do anything in the world, because I had finally gotten somewhere I never thought I could get and I did it on my own. I achieved the impossible. I had thought that it was impossible and it wasn't."

I said, "Deep down you knew you could do it, and you manifested it."

To which she replied, "I did know it deep down and I did manifest it. I gave up everything, I gave up my apartment, and got rid of all my things. I was preparing for this in every capacity. I sold all my furniture, I rented a locker, saved what I deemed worth saving, went to zero expenses. Just my cell phone and my locker. And everything else went straight to savings. So when I bought in 2014 I had only been travelling for a year and a little bit and I saved $33,000. I banked it all. Still I don't even know how I did it. I didn't even look at the money, I just did it."

Marcella had the desire for the dream, she set the goal and took action, remained persistent, and committed then took the opportunity when it came.

"She played with the intention of winning where others play trying to make sure to not lose."

Many home buyers are afraid they will lose money but Marcella wasn't. She was doing this for her financial security and other reasons. Her thoughts never involved loss. She did not allow me or anyone else to keep her from achieving her goal. Once she had set her mind to it she was determined to get it. She played with the intention of winning where others play trying to make sure to not lose. That's a confusing sentence and it's worth re-reading it. There's a big difference. One is a confident position, a clearly defined goal with the knowledge that you can do it, the other is a fear-based position and a limiting belief.

Top 14 Ways to Build Self-Confidence to Buy Your Own Home
1. Set short-term goals and achieve them as this will rewire your brain for success. Set a goal to save a specific amount of money, for example.
2. Celebrate your accomplishments, reward yourself and you will develop the habit of succeeding.
3. Define your personal values (i.e. independence, security).
4. List your strengths, such as budgeting, planning, being open minded, researching.
5. Practise adapting and looking for opportunity instead of focusing on negative roadblocks.
6. Recall a time you overcame objection or a negative situation. Write down how you did it and think of how you can use the same technique for your home purchase journey.
7. Take control of your thoughts and focus on positive thoughts.
8. Set the clearly defined goal, know exactly what you want and why.
9. Commit to the goal. Make a serious commitment to do everything in your own power to succeed. A strong commitment will allow you to easily overcome obstacles.

10. Set the action plan starting with manageable tasks like checking your credit score, saving 10 per cent of each pay cheque, visiting the neighbourhoods you wish to buy into.
11. Visualize yourself as a homeowner, feel the emotions you will feel.
12. Create daily rituals that help you stay positive.
13. Find the key in awareness. When we can identify the belief that holds us back and causes us pain we can release it and move past it.
14. Start today by doing something that will start you on your journey. It doesn't matter what it is, no matter how small, just do it. By taking the first step right now you will be on the right path.

CHAPTER 6

Building Wealth through Real Estate

In 2011, I left *Property Virgins* and had pitched the network a show idea I had created called *Buy Herself*. It was about single women buying real estate. When I told the network that one in four buyers was a single female, and only 1 in 10 were single men, they were very intrigued. I had always found it interesting that I worked with many more single women of all ages and walks of life but only a few single men. I thought it was because I was a woman and that women like to work with female realtors, however the statistic became available through NAR and the sociologist in me latched onto this new info.

Around that time, I was opening up my own brokerage in Toronto and had scouted out an office furniture store close by. I visited the store several times and got to know the woman who was running the business. She pointed me in the direction of some Herman Miller designs and I had a lot of fun planning out the office space in a manner that would make it inviting to consumers and also a great place to work and hang out.

She was very knowledgeable and helpful. I loved that she had just gotten a large breed puppy that she brought to the office with her every day. Puppies are amazing loving creatures who are always ready to play, give kisses, and accept back rubs. They really exude joie de vivre that is enviable. Puppies are full of positive energy and just want to love and play and explore. Just like humans they can grow to be angry and aggressive, timid or well balanced. This depends on their conditioning and how they were taught to be. Quite often a vicious dog is a scared dog and a dog who has fear will often be aggressive. I've learned that people operate the same way.

The last time I was at the store she started asking me questions about being a realtor, how to get licensed, how much it cost and what it was like to be a salesperson. I get those questions often, but she was asking in a way that seemed a bit unusual for someone who was so engrained in a business already. I asked why she was so curious and she told me that she would be losing her job soon.

She was over fifty years old at that time and had been running the entire business for the owner for the last 20 years or more. She wasn't just a manager, she was running the whole business. The owner had another location that was about an hour and fifteen minutes away and he decided to shut down the Toronto location and run the entire business out of the other location. She wasn't about to move to a new city for a job and she wasn't interested in commuting that far.

> "I'm not worried though, I only have
> two more mortgage payments and
> then I'll own my house outright."

I was shocked and I felt for her. What a horrible situation, to have been so integral to a company for decades and suddenly have to face the reality of being jobless late in your career. She knew she would have a hard time finding a job she liked as much as she liked this one and knew that companies would prefer to hire someone younger and less expensive than she was, so she figured she would just get one or two part-time jobs.

Then she said words that I would love to put on a poster: "I'm not worried though, I only have two more mortgage payments and then I'll own my house outright." After the mortgage was paid off she would only have to pay taxes and utilities, which she could manage with a part time job.

I always tell this story and joke that she should be the spokesperson for *Buy Herself*. How amazing that she had made a decision over 20 years ago that positioned her so well for the unknown circumstances in life. Remember the old expression, life happens while you are busy making plans? She never would have guessed 20 years before that she would be a few years away from retirement when she would see her career come to a grinding halt.

Property owners have options

Had she been renting all those years, she would now be faced with having to pay rent regardless of being unemployed. To rent a place like her house she'd pay about $2,500 per month plus utilities and she might have a hard time finding a landlord that would take on a large dog. Now that she would no longer have a full-time job she would not have the option of purchasing a home with a mortgage as lenders would want proof that she would be able to pay the mortgage.

Thankfully, by purchasing a home she had given herself options in her life. She could sell her fully detached house and downsize to something smaller with lower property taxes and heating bills. She could move to a smaller house, a townhouse, a less expensive semi-detached house or a condo apartment if those options would put some money in the bank while allowing her to maintain home ownership.

She could rent out a portion of her house to gain some passive income. If she wanted to rent out a room in her house periodically, perhaps on Airbnb or short term to college students, she could gain a bit of income. If she didn't like the idea of sharing her personal space and was concerned about privacy and safety she could consider renting out the self-contained and separate basement apartment to a permanent tenant. She could move to the basement and rent out the main floor and upper to a family who would pay more money. The laws in her municipality allow for this kind of activity but it is best to verify that renting is acceptable in your location if you decide to pursue a similar stream of passive income.

She could continue to live in the house working part-time to pay the bills, which were about $8,000 per year. She would be able to take equity out of the house to pay for a new roof or furnace, or just budget wisely for those expenses. Homeowners should put money aside each month to be able to cover the expenses of replacing roof, furnace, and air conditioning especially if they are older.

Had she never purchased the house she would be faced with the challenge of having to pay rent and utilities amounting to $35,000 per year rather than the $8,000 year she was facing. She may not have been able to have her beautiful puppy and her lifestyle may have been affected. She would constantly be stressed by her financial situation unless she had planned extremely well for her retirement. Many experts will tell you that very few people plan effectively for retirement and given the fact that it came on unexpectedly early the issue would have been amplified.

Options. She had options. I told you about the TV judge berating a woman for having put herself in a situation where she didn't have options. The judge basically told her that she had willingly backed into that corner herself. She had done nothing proactively to give herself options. Fortunately, this woman had opened up the door to so many options that she could easily navigate her future the way she wanted to.

I constantly think about how real estate can help people and how it is possible to purchase and own property and how it would provide options for them. Life can be so unpredictable and we can never know what our lives will be like a year from now, five years or 20 years from now. The TV judge's advice to this woman has been on my mind ever since I saw that segment and I often retell the story to my clients and potential clients. My hope is that they will see just how important it can be to own real estate as their principal residence and investment properties. This woman's story demonstrates how paying your mortgage off can put you in a pretty sweet position and prepare you for some of life's curveballs even if you can't ever imagine them coming at you.

Let's say she had only been a homeowner for half the time, say 10 years and had only paid off about half of her mortgage principal amount. In Toronto over the last 30 years, the property values have increased 5 per cent annually. That includes a big correction in 1989 and a couple of other corrections up to and including 2018.

Let's say in 2008 she had purchased an average-priced home in Toronto. In Toronto, the benchmark price for a 2-storey detached home in September 2018 was $1,253,500 as reported by the Toronto Real Estate Board on the Home Price Index report. That price is slightly more than double what it was 10 years earlier. So, you could say the benchmark price was about $628,000 in 2008. So even if she had never paid down one dime toward her loan amount she would have made $628,000 in tax free dollars from her principal residence.

But wait, the numbers are even better when you take into account that she's paid off almost half of her mortgage by making payments every two weeks instead of one time per month. By doing this she pays her mortgage off about 4.4 years faster. So now she has about $300,000 paid off plus the $628,000 she made on the value of the house for a total of $928,000. It cost her money every month to live there but she would have paid out 10 years of rent during that time and in my opinion it's a wash. Even if she could have rented for less than what her principal and interest cost, she'd still be ahead.

Let's say she made $40,000 worth of improvements over the years with a new roof, new furnace, new A/C unit, new bathroom and some paint, etc. or even if she had renovated at the expense of $150,000 she still is way better off financially (and her house could be worth more than the benchmark price if she did smart renovations that were well executed). You could argue that if she had invested money in a retirement fund or in equities, she could make that kind of money in 10 years. Of course, it's taxable income when you use the money from retirement savings and stocks, and to be honest, who the hell has the discipline and the luck to make that kind of money? Not enough people, that's who. By the way, home ownership does not preclude you from investing in stocks and retirement funds, you could do both and make money from both of these investment vehicles. You may not want to keep all of your money in real estate but I recommend that you consider investing in property. According to property agency Knight Frank, "multi-millionaire families in North America have 34 per cent of their wealth in real estate, excluding their principal home."[2]

Toronto is where I live and work however this principal can be used with housing in other markets. The chart included here demonstrates

2   Erica Alini, "Is too much of your wealth tied up in the housing market?" *Global News*, Jan. 17, 2019. https://globalnews.ca/news/4844683/ housing-market-wealth-investment/

how much money you can make on an investment property. You can make money with just one investment property.

INVESTMENT PROPERTY

Year	Value	Growth*	Increase	New Value
1	$650,000	8%	$52,000	$702,000
2	$702,000	8%	$56,160	$758,160
3	$758,160	8%	$60,653	$818,830
4	$818,830	8%	$65,505	$884,335
5	$884,335	8%	$70,747	$955,082

*Growth rate is not guaranteed however CREA reports 10.4% national average April 2017

**3.5% interest rate used in example above; 25 year amortization, monthly payments. Rates vary and you should consult your Premiere Relationship Manager for up-to-date information. Example shown is for illustrative purposes only and does not constitute a recommendation to purchase or sell real estate for investment purposes.

RECAP

- Purchase price $650,000
- Initial Investment (20%) $130,000
- Appreciation over 5 yrs $305,065
- Tenants pay principal $71,344 (3.5%)**
- Potential Increase in Net Worth over 5 yrs $376,409
  - 10 yrs $909,505
  - 20 yrs $2,756,821

*Growth rate is not guaranteed however CREA reports 10.4% national average April 2017

**3.5% interest rate is used in example above; 25 year amortization, monthly payments. Rates vary and you should consult your Premiere Relationship Manager for up-to-date information.. Example shown is for illustrative purposes only and does not constitute a recommendation to purchase or sell real estate for investment purposes.

I think of real estate as a long-term investment. You can renovate and flip houses, you buy and assign, work rent to own homes, you can gamble in the real estate market and many people make money doing that. I'm not talking about that in this book, because I've seen too many people take risks and lose money, relationships, and energy playing a short-term investment game. Some expensive courses are being sold to the public that teach you how to become a real estate investor. Many of them will tell you that you need a large number of properties in order to build wealth in real estate. Many of those courses teach six strategies for investing in property:

Six Strategies

1. Wholesaling or Assignments
   An investor ties up a property and then tries to resell it at a profit, or entices other people to buy it as a partnership.
2. Flipping
   You've seen the TV shows. An investor buys a property that would potentially increase in value with some renovations and upgrades and does the work in a short period of time hoping to gain a profit.
3. Become Licensed Realtor
   They tell you to get your license so you can buy and sell properties and earn income on the commissions.
4. Become Property Manager
   They advise that you could become a property manager for the investors you've set up with investment properties.
5. Rent-to-Own
   You find people who are unable to buy a home at this time and rent to them at a higher price. All parties plan to transfer title to the tenants on a specified date.
6. Buy and Hold
   This is what I refer to as the long game. Buy property and gain equity as the value increases and the tenant pays your mortgage down.

Do your research on these courses if you are considering taking one. Some of them offer a $3,000 weekend teaser course and then get you to sign up for their $20,000 course to find out their deepest secrets. Personally, I think you can do very well with just one or two investment properties. I believe the average person can make money owning just their principal residence and many will be happy with that, others still will want to invest. Many baby boomers are buying condos as investments because they see the value in real estate. They may wish to house their parents in the condo, keep it for the kids, or rent it out.

Buy something that will be easy to sell if you ever have to liquidate quickly

When you buy real estate it's important to make sure you buy something that will be easy to sell if you ever have to liquidate quickly. Avoid special properties, the ones that have unique floor plans or features that the majority of people shy away from. Remember this: average sells. Don't buy the biggest house/condo in the area unless you really want that prestige or space for yourself. Your investment will not appreciate at the same rate as the average house or condo so from a purely investment perspective it's not the best allocation of your funds.

Don't add in over the top finishes or over-improve for the area. Many buyers are on a budget and want to buy a house with space and location that suits their needs. They may not want to pay for fancy technology or over the top landscaping and may choose a more reasonably priced property over yours. This often holds true even in the luxury market.

Avoid stigmatized properties because if you have to sell in a slow market you may find yourself unable to effect a sale. A stigmatized property is one that buyers shun because of reasons other than physical attributes of the property, for example houses where a murder has been committed or one that backs on to electrical towers.

Smaller houses and condos appreciate faster and get more money per square foot than large ones, but micro condos may be problematic. At this time, only a handful of lenders will finance a micro condo, making them more difficult to resell. In Toronto co-ops are not the best money makers and banks view them as risky because of the way ownership is defined. Lenders tend to avoid lending on them unless the buyer has a very large down payment. If the bank finds them risky you had better find out why and decide if you are willing to take the risk.

Hire a professional

To know your market, hire a professional who knows everything you need to know and who will be able and willing to communicate it to you in a manner you can understand. One who welcomes questions and loves to share their extensive knowledge with their clients.

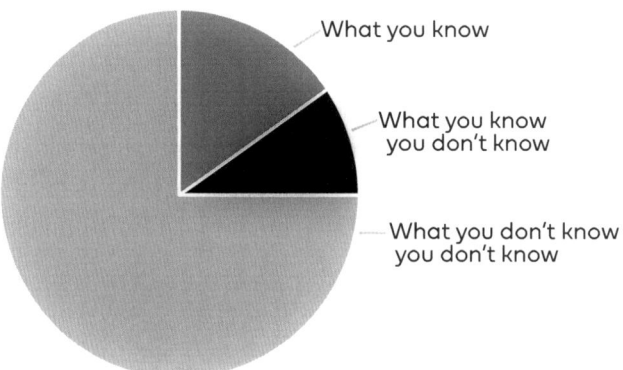

You can research, read, view TV shows like my own, and learn a lot about real estate but you'll never know as much as an expert unless you dedicate your life to becoming an expert yourself. The pie graph shows you that you should be wise enough to know that you don't know everything there is to know about real estate investing. (If you don't know that yet you will find out the hard way.) There is a portion of the pie that illustrates what you know and what you know you don't know. The largest portion of the pie shows what you don't know you don't know. That's where a sharp professional comes in. They must know everything within that category so that they can lead you well or at least be willing to find out whatever they are lacking knowledge in.

Even a newer realtor with limited experience can still work to your benefit provided they have the support they need from a mentor or broker, and they aren't afraid to ask. After 24 years, I still don't know everything I need to know. I won't stop learning because every day something new comes up, some new type of property, technology, construction system, market conditions and regulations change and so much more. If I'm going to be the best that I can be for my clients and to mentor real estate salespeople I will have to keep learning. Luckily, I love learning! I'm one of those people who will continue to read, watch documentaries, and learn until I die.

When you buy real estate investments you should understand what your intentions are so that you can accomplish the goal more efficiently. You could purchase property that would provide a positive cash flow and income for you. You could purchase property that would not yield a great income for you immediately but is located in an area that would appreciate at a very good rate and would increase in value. Do you want cash flow or do you want deferred funds? It's a choice of income or equity. Know what your desired outcome is before you begin the process.

If you buy with a partner or partners be sure to have an exit strategy in place before you begin. You won't be caught unawares should your partnership dissolve or if one partner wants to cash out. Know your options and what they will cost you. Settling this at the beginning of the partnership will help to avoid some unnecessary nastiness later.

CHAPTER 7

Just Because She Wanted To

It's hard to break from tradition.

I had to pleasure to work with a lovely woman who was living at home with her parents. In her late thirties she had taken on the role of daughter quite zealously and would vacuum, clean, and do housework and the males in the household wouldn't lift a finger. These are traditional roles for the demographic. Girls were expected to stay home until they were married, girls helped Mom with the traditional women's tasks like cooking, cleaning, and running the household and Dev didn't mind at all.

I met Dev after a long-term relationship had ended. She explained that she had looked forward to owning a home with her future partner so they could have a great place to raise a family, much like her own childhood home. Once the relationship ended she never held on to the dream of home ownership.

Dev had heard me speaking on a popular radio station talking about how women are disrupting the real estate market. She told me that when she heard the segment she thought, "Wait, what? Women buy real estate on their own?" She started to think about it for the first time and wondered why she had never thought about it before now. She had believed that just because she wanted it wasn't a big enough reason to have it. WHOAH! It is the *only* reason! There doesn't have to be a reason why you want to buy real estate other than because you want to. She had possessed the confidence to break up an engagement and now she was developing the courage to buy a home on her own. This girl was going to bust out of the box!

She had never moved out before and nobody in her family had ever bought a home on their own without a spouse or family, not a man and not a woman. Her idea of moving out was already going to challenge the beliefs of the family but committing to home ownership was taking it to the extreme. She was nervous about what her family would think.

Don't hold back on your dreams!

She had never given any thought to what kind of life she could have other than becoming a wife and mother. This was a big step for Dev. The first time you really allow yourself to dream you usually hold yourself back in many ways. Dev was concerned about what her family would say, and she didn't want to let them down. That caused her to focus on buying a home that was close to the family home. A family member she respected thought it would be better to stay within the comfort zone and to take baby steps by getting a house near the family. The well-intentioned family member wanted her to play small and was unknowingly teaching Dev to be afraid. She was in the protector role and while she did not try to dissuade Dev she was inadvertently holding her back and putting limits on her dreams.

The friends at work on the other hand told her to create a new life and go downtown to a young urban vibe. She started to envision her life outside of the family-oriented subdivision and with people who shared her interests. This represented a bigger change and was frightening yet exciting.

Dev was no wallflower. One thing I noticed about Dev from the start was when she walked into a property she was empowered, she was like, "Yeah, I'm going to check out this place!" She was walking in a determined manner without hesitation and with confidence. Body language is something a good realtor learns to pick up on, but the truth is we all pick up on it even if we don't recognize our ability and we all react or respond to it.

After she had toured a condo the process had become a reality to her and she had begun to see that there was more out there than she had ever considered. She opened her mind to new possibilities and you could almost see the cloak of tradition fall from her shoulders. It was amazing and I'm so grateful that I got to witness this and to help a little in the process. Dev was determined to see more possibilities and find out what was right for her.

We toured houses in her family neighbourhood, and we toured downtown condos. She was torn between two worlds, traditional family area with similar housing type to her family home and modern condo living for which she had no reference point, no experience to draw upon. Branching out was causing her some anxiety and although she loved the uber modern downtown condo she was having trouble seeing herself there. She was clinging, as many of us do, to what was familiar even though it may or may not have been the best for her.

Go ahead – be the first

Without any role models to follow she would have to lead the way. She was the first and that presented its challenges as she second guessed herself along the way. She had to learn to stop giving priority to the world she thought and had to give priority to the world she desired.

> "Connection is why we're here. We are hardwired to connect with others, it's what gives purpose and meaning to our lives, and without it there is suffering."[3] —Brené Brown

---

3 Brené Brown, *Daring Greatly: How the Courage to Be Vulnerable Transforms the Way We Live, Love, Parent, and Lead* (New York: Avery, 2015).

One thing some people worry about is what will make a certain person happy or what that person will think. It comes from our need to fit in, to belong. Many experts suggest that we are hardwired for a deep sense of belonging and connecting. The result is we change our personality in order to fit in to a group. When you are constantly trying to fit in, to be accepted, to feel like you belong you make changes to your personality. You pretend to like things you don't, to be things you are not and you suppress your real feelings in order to fit in with everyone else. That is how we end up putting ourselves into the box. We don't allow ourselves to think outside the box because we would risk judgment and risk losing our place in the cool kids group. You don't want to be the weird kid who eats lunch by herself because nobody wants to sit with her. They could become labelled as weird too and that would be too much to bear.

The expression we all know, "If you don't have anything nice to say don't say anything at all", is debilitating! We are taught that we should not express ourselves or express our true beliefs. It's yet another way to keep us inside the box and it comes from tradition and years of conditioning. The truth is we can think one way while accepting those who think another way.

Dev was able to find her true desire. She was able to stop worrying about what will make this or that person happy or what they would think. She was able to shift her focus to her own dream, her own desires and she didn't let go of it even when things became more challenging. Buying a place appears to be the goal but making yourself happy is the real goal. A goal like home ownership allows you to grow and to become your true self.

> "Once you realize that you hold the key you will never allow yourself to be incarcerated again."

We allow ourselves to live in a jail cell and we can see that the door to the cell is open but we are too afraid to take a step outside and free ourselves. Once Dev took the step she felt like a rebel because she did it simply because she wanted to. That was very empowering for her and I'm sure the newly found power found its way into many aspects of her life, transforming her from a woman bound by tradition to a free-thinking person. Once you realize that you hold the key you will never allow yourself to be incarcerated again.

Dev learned to dream and to really think. Not to just respond to conditioning without thought as she had done repeatedly. She really thought about what she wanted and had the courage to make a decision. Once the decision was made, action was taken and the goal, the dream, was achieved.

None of these women that I write about have suffered the heinous crimes that we think about happening around the world. We tend to think they happen half way around the world, but they are happening in our country, our cities. In some families, girls have no value at all. And when something has no value you treat it without respect, with no regard. The women in these pages may not have suffered the horrendous crimes against their freedom and body but their challenges were difficult to overcome nonetheless. No matter what material the cell bars are made of you feel like you can't get out.

It might be said that women are always thinking of others, that we are soft and loving. In order to fulfill this belief we often shrink ourselves so that our partner, boss, parent, sibling will not feel threatened, will not experience any negative feelings. If I am too (insert word of your choice here) they won't love me. We sacrifice ourselves and our needs to allow someone else to feel better. I worked with a client who had to be very careful not to buy a better property than her older sibling owned even though she could afford and would have loved to buy a more expensive property. This tradition was part of their culture and she would not break tradition even though it meant that she had to sacrifice her own desires.

"Repeatedly holding back to spare
someone's feelings is not healthy and does
not allow you to live your true self."

The idea of repeatedly holding back to spare someone's feelings is not healthy and does not allow you to live your true self. In this situation, you may delude yourself that you are a giving person and you don't mind stepping into the shadow so they will feel less threatened, that you are being loving or that you are so secure in yourself that you don't mind. You may say it is your culture that dictates the behaviour. That's just lip service, something we tell ourselves so that we can justify living a small life and to justify controlling ourselves. We rationalize staying in the jail cell that we have created for ourselves and to avoid causing a commotion we close our eyes to the fact that the door is wide open. We don't allow ourselves to flourish, to create, to expand and we believe it is okay to do so. We believe this because we have learned to believe it. Someone has conditioned us to think this way.

Dev's story really resonated with me. Here she was, beautiful, healthy, intelligent and yet she hadn't allowed herself to blossom into everything she wanted to be. Well, there's the key word, *want*. She hadn't allowed herself to want a home. She believed she would get all of that with a partner. She was satisfied with following the traditions laid out for her during her upbringing. It was safe, it was expected of her, and she was the type to follow the tradition so as not to create waves. What she wanted did not factor into the program mostly because she didn't allow herself to explore with dreams.

She had been involved in a serious relationship with plans to marry and one day she realized that although she loved this man it wasn't the love it would take for a marriage to endure. So she took the steps to break up the engagement. I mean WOW, that takes courage! When I was getting married the first time I knew deep down it wasn't right but I didn't allow the knowledge to surface. I was afraid to acknowledge that truth. I didn't have the courage to face the fact that we weren't right together as spouses. That was a mountain of emotional garbage I just wasn't prepared to climb at that time. That heap of trash was my conditioning, and I allowed it to hold me back. My upbringing taught me that if you were a good wife, if you cooked, cleaned and raised the kids you'd have a successful marriage. Where is my happiness in that formula? I tell you where, NOwhere. I wasn't raised to think of my own happiness, good Lord no! It wasn't even on the list. What the hell is that? How do you raise children without thinking, *I just want them to be happy*?

Well, it's not as simple as that, really. I mean, parents have traditions and beliefs from their own upbringing that may become outdated and never updated, almost like they have been living in a time capsule. They come over with their experiences in the old country and hold on to the belief that nothing ever changes. They come with a time capsule of mores, traditions, and a way of life.

I once heard Sadhguru say, "Tradition is often an anchor that we hold on to for stability or confidence." He explains that what someone did yesterday is today's culture and tradition. What you do today will be tomorrow's tradition. Not everything we do is perfect but time will make it seem so to future generations and that may cause problems.

Are you familiar with the story called *The Lottery* by Shirley Jackson? The town takes part in a macabre activity each year simply because that is the way it had always been done. Each member of the town is registered and must pull a slip of paper from an old black box. The box is shabby but they dare not replace it because they are afraid to mess with tradition. The person who selects the slip of paper with a black dot on it gets stoned to death. Of course, it doesn't make any sense at all yet the tradition is so deep in their society that they believe that letting go of it would result in a backward step in human development. This is their anchor, their stability.

Perhaps you have heard the story of the woman who cut the legs off the turkey when she was preparing to put it in the oven. Someone watching her asked her why she did that but she didn't know why she did it. All she knew was that she saw her mom do that every year. She called her mom to ask why she did that and she said that it was because she didn't have a roaster big enough to hold the whole turkey so she removed the legs to make it fit. At that point the woman realized that she could stop removing the turkey legs because her roaster was large enough to hold the entire bird. When an authoritative figure espouses it we accept it. That is unconscious living and we are going through motions without thinking.

When some of the Italians that came over in the 1950s went back to Italy after several years for the first time, they got the shock of their lives when they found out there was a drug problem and they discovered that many Italian women didn't know how to cook, that they were pursuing careers or jobs and not getting married at a young age nor having a ton of kids. It wasn't the Italy they remembered.

Their entire belief system was rocked and rolled and broken. Many of them didn't allow it to be broken up so they didn't have to start new. Instead, they made excuses, saying those women were not from Italy, or they were from another part of Italy (which is not as good as their part of course), or some other lie that helped them skip past the evidence so they wouldn't have to change their perception. They would rather change the evidence than change their belief. Think about that for a moment. You live inside this time capsule if you will, and you pass on to your kids what you know. Right? I mean, my mom was a stay-at-homer and her job was to make sure the kids didn't mess up. We were three girls and none of us got into any serious trouble.

Find a way to feel happy and fulfilled

Well, I ran away twice but one time was only for two hours. I went to the park down the street with my dog Prince and waited for the search party that never came. Anyway, in that type of environment you want the best for your kids and since getting married and raising the kids, cooking and being a good wife worked for my mom she figured that it had to work for me too. She never considered that she may not have been entirely happy and that life didn't really work for her. It never occurred to her that since times actually had changed maybe she could dig a little deeper to examine the formula and find some way to make herself happy and fulfilled. She never did, so I never dreamed I was missing something and should try to fulfill my own needs and desires. That's how the paradigm is passed to children. The intent is to make sure the kids are all right and since the parents only know one way of life they expect it to be what the children need. Some people would truly be happy in that lifestyle because it is what they dream of and what they really want. I take issue with limiting the dreams of children. Let them dream, let them strive for whatever it is they want.

In my first marriage I was terribly unhappy. For me to actually admit that the relationship wasn't what I wanted or needed or could make a success out of was just too much to take on at that time. I didn't have any experience with asking for what I wanted nor did I even know what I wanted. I didn't know that I actually had value and should dream about the possibilities that life could offer.

The power to choose

Girls of my generation and background didn't learn that they had the power to choose, that they had value, could achieve and succeed, could create their own happiness however they envisioned it. If you ever dreamed of having a career you had to deal with the paradigms of others. They'd warn that you could be the CEO but shouldn't forget that you have to do everything a proper stay-at-home mom would do as well. Your silly little career should never get in the way of bringing up baby even if you are the main earner in your household.

Dev had experienced an upbringing that didn't really open up the door to thinking outside the box. Her career was a safe one for women, bank teller. Many of the working daughters of immigrants worked at a bank as a teller because it was a job that was acceptable for women. You would never strive to be the CFO or CEO of the bank. Dev had parents who wanted the best for her and to them the best was the life they had lived. She was expected to live with her parents until she was married and would move into a house with her husband.

She didn't even think about getting a home on her own, because nobody, no woman in her entire family had ever bought real estate on her own. She didn't know she could or should buy alone until she heard me heard me during an interview talking about women buying real estate. She was not afraid of taking emotional risk. She had already taken a huge risk emotionally by ending her relationship. She had achieved her own happiness in doing so. For Dev, it was about thinking outside the box, about looking at potential that had not been part of her learning experiences growing up. As soon as she heard about women buying real estate she was on board. For Dev, it was about figuring out what she wanted in property.

The word condo wasn't even in her vocabulary when she talked about real estate. She had only ever lived in a house, her family members had houses. A condo was not within her references and we tend to strive for what we know, what we have seen or experienced. Alternatively, had she live in apartments or condos all her life she would have struggled with the thought of purchasing a house because that would have been outside her reference.

She only knew houses and had never given thought to leaving the neighbourhood. When she opened her eyes to the possibility of living downtown, with a more urban lifestyle in a pedestrian-friendly area she latched on to it quickly. Once she allowed herself to dream of possibilities, to dream of a new lifestyle, she was successful in choosing, offering on and buying her dream home.

Our personalities are shaped by our beliefs

It can be very difficult to recognize our behaviour as being taught behaviour. We all have personalities and that has something to do with it, right? But even our personalities are shaped by our beliefs. Your thoughts are programmed for you by society, culture, tradition, politics, money, and more. Every moment of every day that we interact with a human we are being conditioned and we are conditioning another human.

When your thoughts are about how your words or actions might make someone else feel, and you hold back and do not say or act the way you would really like to you are responding to false beliefs and allowing external influences to affect your internal being. At the beginning of this journey, Dev had been concerned about what her family would think and she didn't want to upset them. She learned that they were very supportive of her and she discovered that the box she had kept herself in was created and maintained by her, and no one else. It helped that she was a confident woman and one way to build your confidence is to go inside yourself.

Meditation – the quiet journey within

Meditating allows us to discard the outside world and take a trip inside. It can be challenging to meditate if you are not familiar with the practise. You may be afraid of the word or have an issue with it so just call it quiet time. It's important to perform some sort of quiet time meditation if you wish to understand who you really are. Whenever the incessant chatter stops in your head (you're not worthy, you are not capable, not smart enough, not lovable) the magic happens. Try to tap into this daily and every split second that you have a still mind you will be connected to your true self. Some people say we connect to source, or God, or the Universe. Call it what you will but we all agree that it is a connection to the inner you, the real you, your true self.

Your true self believes that all people have value, believes that you should stand up for your rights, believes that you are capable, believes that you are limitless in what you can achieve. Your true self is beautiful, loving, loved, and limitless.

A woman can achieve whatever she
wants to achieve without limitation.

CHAPTER 8

'Wait for Him to Show Up?

Fatima, a beautiful 25-year-old woman, was virtually deposited on her parents' doorstep in Vancouver BC and as she says, "I had nothing. No job, no money, none of my stuff, it was all on a different continent. I was broken. I had no self-esteem. I didn't understand how I had gotten here after such a short time."

As a child, she had lived in a middle-class home with a traditional family with siblings. She was in the middle of the pack in age and she was "the good child". She never talked back, always followed the rules, didn't drink or carry on, never got into trouble in the community, and was a very good student. She always had food, shelter, and love.

Her parents had a very traditional marriage that followed the ways of the past. In their culture men and women had their men and women had their roles carved out by years of tradition. The expectations were expressed openly and also in a more subtle fashion. Girls like Fatima knew what kind of life lay ahead and she simply accepted it and never questioned it.

When Fatima was accepted to a Vancouver university, she didn't really want to go. She hadn't been motivated to get a university degree, she was fine with perhaps going to two years of college and getting a college diploma. Fatima's mother was not having it. Fatima recalls that although her father did not believe it was necessary or important that Fatima go to school, and challenged the notion, her mother was adamant that she go to university. "She has been accepted to university and has a scholarship so she is going to university!" Off she went, 20 minutes away of course, as she was not allowed to leave her parents' home to go off to university, as it simply was not accepted in her household. She had to stay home, there was no option to go away to school. She earned a four-year Honours BA in Sociology.

§§§

This upbringing is so similar to mine you could almost insert my name wherever you see Fatima. Some subtle differences of course, my background is Italian and my mother didn't actually push me to go to university. Instead she encouraged me to get a job as a secretary and marry my boss. In a sense she in fact inadvertently pushed me to apply to University by showing me my certain destiny.

During this time frame the mother's responsibility in a Mediterranean household was to raise the kids and keep them out of trouble. If one of my two sisters or I messed up Mom would be to blame. It was in my mother's best interest to marry me off young and pass this responsibility on to my husband. In other words, as Fatima says, "secure the girls!" It's kind of boiling it down to its crudest form but that was the underlying sentiment.

I believed this was my destiny, because my mother had said so. After all, she knew me well, she knew what I was capable of and she said this was what I could aim for.

§§§

After completing university, Fatima felt she could no longer stay in her hometown. She said she didn't want to be a woman who was just sitting around waiting for a "him", a husband to show up at her parents' house. She wanted more, she wanted to live, to experience a more exciting life outside of her hometown, away from her parents' watchful eye. She told her parents she was just going to visit her brothers, but she never went back. She had been working in retail and had asked for a transfer closer to where her uncle lived. She packed up her stuff and moved to live with her uncle and his family as he was the cool uncle. While her dad was upset he was consoled by the fact that she was living with extended family with a male family member as head of the household. She was safe and he could rely on them to keep her in line.

Fatima did well at work and was promoted and offered positions around the country. When she accepted her first transfer her Dad was very upset and refused to acknowledge her desire to have a career. He thought, she had a good job, she was safe, she didn't need advancement in her career so why couldn't she just be happy and stay put until she got married? He believed that what she had was good enough and she should not strive for more.

Of course, he would not have said these things to either of his sons. The expectations for boys are very different; the rules, the road, the things boys are allowed to dream and do are very different from what daughters are allowed.

An opportunity to live on her own!

She had climbed high in the corporate environment and had achieved more than she ever imagined she would. She was thrilled to be able to move around the country and live in cities she had only heard of, never having travelled within Canada. She had to try it out! There was no way she wasn't going to seize the opportunity to live on her own, and in a strange city to boot!

She gave it a go for a while but found it difficult to manage on the low wages. The job didn't pan out and being alone was difficult. Having no regrets, she's proud that she did it, she had lived on her own in fabulous cities, she had given it a shot. She didn't allow this to be a negative that would influence her decisions going forward but rather felt proud that she had tried it and then moved on having learned a few lessons and having strengthened her resolve.

Fatima moved back in with her uncle and his family and began job hunting immediately. Before she knew it she had a new job and had fallen in love too! After a short whirlwind romance she was married.

I wondered why she would marry so quickly seeing as she was independent and wasn't in a rush to move out of the parents' house as she was already out. She explained that she married him because she loved him so much and wanted to be his wife. Although there wasn't a need to get out of the house there was some pressure to get married for stability. For parents in her culture "the goal was to secure the girls so the girls are no longer their problem," she said.

The pressure was there, both subtle and not so subtle, from the family, from the community, and from within. Fatima felt that marriage was the path to security for women in her culture. The groom's family lived in overseas so he landed a job there and Fatima had to move to overseas. Everyone felt it was a good opportunity for the newlyweds. They would work a few years, save a lot of money then move back to Canada and buy a house. That was the plan so Fatima had to uproot her life to marry him and move to another continent.

The first year of marriage was difficult and as Fatima said, the odds were against them at that point because they barely knew each other, they were young and barely knew themselves, they were living in a foreign country, and she had no support from family or friends. Every day, she would watch hours of television programs. She was bored, she was not used to this kind of life. She was used to being independent, coming and going, doing things.

He had his family there, he had a big support system of family and friends but Fatima didn't know anyone. When problems started happening she had no one to go to. Her parents grew very concerned for her, as they were too far away to be able to help their daughter with the problems she was having in her marriage.

Culture clashes

There were cultural differences between the bride and groom. He had been born in the Middle East and she had been raised in Canada. He had grown up in a traditional Middle Eastern family. He had married an independent forward-thinking woman and suddenly wanted to convert her into a subservient wife with no equality in the relationship. His mother had advised Fatima to greet her husband with made up, beautifully dressed and to treat him like he was a King, get his slippers for him and make sure the house was exactly the way he liked it, with or without his favourite music playing, ask him how his day was and to never bother him with her own issues. When Fatima laughed it became very clear that this was not the response the family was hoping for.

Fatima finally landed a job which got her out of the house. It was acceptable for married women to work and this job offered a great opportunity for career advancement.

Her husband's friends teased him about marrying such a beautiful wife and said that he was not worthy of her. He too made comments that when they went out together men looked at him as if wondering how he got this girl. To make things even worse, she had secured a position that was better than his own job. He became threatened by her intelligence and by her education. He started to feel that his manhood was being threatened. He began to lash out at her, desperately trying to overcome his own insecurities by degrading her. He tried to elevate his status by humiliating her. His feelings of superiority were challenged and he reacted by trying to make her feel inferior to him. She had been trying to avoid allowing his paradigms to affect hers and was struggling with it because she had no support.

The couple travelled back to Canada to visit their families. When they arrived there was a big blowout; the families had gotten involved and it had become a disaster. Everyone had their backs up, emotions were running high, nobody was thinking clearly, and the situation spun out of control. Fatima was young and didn't feel confident enough to put her hand in to try to calm down the families, she didn't believe she had the ability to say anything at that point as she had never fought with elders before. In her culture you are taught to respect your elders and to never talk back or challenge them. At best, you secretly packed your bags and left under false pretenses, as she had done when she left the family home years earlier.

She managed to tell her mom that she couldn't deal with this type of existence, that she couldn't imagine putting her future children through this for their entire lives. Her mother backed her and suddenly Fatima had the support she needed to make a change, to save herself. Her father had always tried to act as a buffer between them, explaining to Fatima's husband that she was his blood and he wanted his son-in-law to understand that he wouldn't allow her to be treated badly. He had tried to remain neutral but when he saw first-hand how the family treated his little girl the papa bear version of him appeared. He backed his daughter and let it be known that she was going to stay in Canada. The attacks kept on coming, one attack after another, and it was an ugly divorce. Fatima's husband virtually left her there on her parents' doorstep, with only the clothes on her back.

She sat in her parent's basement and wondered how the heck she had ended up where she was. She had bought in to the story that if you are a good girl and a good wife you will be happy but it hadn't worked. She felt like she had nothing except debt. She had come for a visit with a suitcase of clothes and that was all she had. The rest of her stuff was overseas. She had some debt left over from paying for part of the wedding.

She was feeling dispirited. She was depressed. She couldn't show her face in the community, she was afraid to run into someone she knew. She was embarrassed to explain what had happened, why she was back in town separated from her brand new husband after only a short time. She felt like a complete failure, she felt like she had nothing going for her. She cut off all social media. She knew that people were more concerned about the entertainment of gossiping about her story rather than really caring about her. She chopped her long gorgeous thick hair off and shaved the back of her head to physically if not symbolically change herself.

She started to build a new life, took a job in Toronto, and left her parents' basement after only two months. Her ex-husband had tried to get her back for about a year. He fully expected her to be pining away in the basement, had expected her to accept his apology and false promises. With her family supporting her, Fatima was able to resist and held on to her self-respect with determination.

Doing the right thing

She found a basement apartment that was two levels below grade and very dungeon-like. It was full of spiders, it was dark, and she had no furniture . . . no girl's dream. She knew she could survive this after the experiences she had just had and knew she needed to do this, she could feel that it was right for her.

"The day when I moved into the basement apartment after my divorce was one of the worst of my life. I'll never forget it. I stayed there all alone, I cried there, I completely isolated myself there." She is very grateful for the job that allowed her to move out of her parents' house, that got her to Toronto. If she had stayed in Vancouver she would have felt even more defeated.

"I was alone my first night. After all the screaming and the fighting, the divorce, the problems, everyone's involvement it was just so quiet. I needed that, I needed to be alone with my thoughts. I had to let it sink in, it was still so unbelievable."

It hadn't been easy to uproot herself and move overseas. She had had to deal with that a few months before and now she was back but she didn't have money to ship her things back from overseas She didn't even have clothes to wear to work. Her ex wouldn't send her her things. There were no assets, she was in debt, he had closed their joint accounts. She recalls crying at the bank when she discovered that he had emptied her account. "I had loved this guy so much and I married him out of love, what happened that it transpired to this?! I just had to pick up the pieces at that point. I had no choice."

I mentioned to her that some people might say that she really did have a choice, as she could have gone back, for the security, for the money, the Hummer, the BMW, the villa. Fatima was not that shallow and had more self-respect than that. "I come across women like that all the time. They say they wish they had the guts I had to do that, to leave, but they don't because they don't want to go through the challenges of being independent." They have not allowed themselves to dream about their own desires and had not allowed themselves to create a better life where their authentic selves would thrive.

"This killed me. My divorce genuinely took a huge toll on me psychologically, emotionally, financially, and I felt like shit about myself because I kept thinking of where I should have been at my age. I should be pregnant at this point. I'm back to square one with nothing." Although Fatima was shirking the restrictions of tradition she continued to cling to the paradigm at this point. She was feeling like a failure because she hadn't fulfilled the prescribed lifestyle. It took some time for her to find out who she was and what she wanted.

"I needed to rebuild myself as a person." —Fatima

She went underground for a couple years, stayed off of social media, stayed in the city, she did her own thing. She needed to gain confidence and when she felt better about herself she started up with social media: Facebook, Instagram, etc. She said, "I needed to rebuild myself as a person."

"My life really started after my divorce. I lived on my own, I had a great job that spiralled into a career in a completely different industry, which is huge for me even now. I met a bunch of friends at that time, built a great support system, travelled to all-inclusive resorts about three times a year. My dad was wondering what was happening to me, but I didn't care. Deal with it, this is who I am now." She got her dream and being in control of her life made her very happy.

Breaking free of many of the restrictions that had been ingrained in her, the constraints that women were raised with, the expectations that she had believed in and then tossed aside after having been almost crushed by them, she felt that for the first time in her life she was free to live as she wished. There was nobody to tell her how to live her life, what choices to make and she grew into a strong determined woman.

"The reality is, we hold ourselves back."

"I felt like, I got the job and the apartment because I had to. I can't sit and slum it in my parents' basement, what the hell kind of life is that? I needed to do this, my job was a blessing. It catapulted me in my life, everything else was a result of that. If I didn't get that job I don't know where I would be. It forced me to move to a new city. It forced me to get back up and start socializing again." She felt like it was the first time that she was free to live as she wished, but really she could have done it sooner had she recognized the paradigms that had been holding her back. We hold ourselves back and although we may believe that it is the circumstance that holds us back the reality is, we hold ourselves back.

Fatima is now married and has a small child. "I had no interest in getting married, so there was no rush at all. We took our time until we were ready." The pressure was off because she had already followed the prescription for life that her culture provided and because she was stronger now and living her true self she could shirk the cloak of tradition and live her life her own way. Loving this man had not forced her to give herself up and clearly she was thriving.

I exclaimed that she had been very courageous to take on risks and adventures in her lifetime. She replied, "I've made some major decisions, some major life changes too. I feel like I need it, if I don't have something big going on with my life I'm bored." When she doesn't have a goal she's dead.

I asked her what made her decide to buy a condo. "I was saving for it because I needed something for myself. This was huge step in my life because to this day, I'm the only one of my siblings who owns something! None of the kids have property, everyone rents. It's just so odd, that I'm the only one who bought. I put money into my RRSP ever since I got out of debt. I paid $500 rent in a shitty apartment, saving everything I could. Then it just accumulated to the point where I knew I was ready."

It had taken Fatima five years to get to that point. She had stayed in basement apartments and then a condo rental over the years, preparing for her home purchase.

"Once I had it in my mind, I never let go. I focused all my efforts on that. I know what I want, I have enough money, I watch these shows, I can do this too, and it would be great for me as a person to grow." We chuckled about that, as I had hosted two of those shows. I loved what I was hearing. Fatima had set a goal with determination and persistence. She thought about it all the time and made financial and lifestyle decisions based on her dream. She used this dream to help her heal from the emotional effects of her marriage and divorce.

"And it is an investment for me, and it's only going to appreciate in value. I still own it! It's for my daughter and now it's making money. Now, if anything ever happens I have my condo in the background, it's there. I don't work now that I have child so my back-up is the condo, it's a nest egg and unfortunately you live in a day and age where you have to protect yourself. I just needed to be smarter moving forward, with the decisions I made in my life."

You can always have a dream

The goal of home ownership not only helped Fatima break free from feelings of failure and depression it also provided her with wealth and financial security. Her story demonstrates that even when you feel like you have nothing you can always have a dream and the pursuit of that dream energizes you and lifts you to places that seem way beyond reasonable expectations at the time. She followed the rules of tradition and suffered greatly but she didn't give up, she didn't just lay around feeling sorry for herself. She didn't just stay inside the jail cell she had created for herself. Instead, she took time to find out who she was and what she wanted and then she went and got it. Her circumstances did not hold her back because she created new ones. She found strength in herself and she let her inside determine her outside circumstances.

She found the good in the experiences of her life that she has labelled as bad. She may never have found her true self had she not experienced the bad marriage and the feeling of destitution. She may never have realized just how wonderful her life could truly become had she never felt pain. I believe that she is a far better mother, friend, daughter, sister, and wife now that she is living her true self.

CHAPTER 9

'Don't Give Your Freedom Away

"True self esteem is finding the source of power within
yourself, the source of life within you. It is the continuous
source of intense power, potential of all form."
—Eckhardt Tolle

We take a role in each interaction we have with another person. Every contact we have with a human is an interaction, even riding an elevator with a stranger is a social interaction. I remember in Sociology at U of T we were given the homework to ride an elevator. When you get into an elevator with other people in it you turn and face the door, look up at the ceiling or down at the floor but always straight ahead toward the doors. For this assignment we were enter an elevator that had people on it and were instructed to turn around and face the other riders. Try it sometime, it's freaky. It changes the interaction immediately and people become very uncomfortable and they react. Some will look away from you to avoid making eye contact, others will try to move closer to the door to attempt to avoid you. Some others will ask if everything is okay, or what your problem is. The point is that even that anonymous elevator ride you take is an interaction and within that interaction you take on a role.

At home you are in the role of daughter, son, mother, father, sibling, or perhaps roommate, partner. We have labels for everything because it seems to help us understand our own role and the role of others. We judge based on the label and the role. Have you ever gone to a function where you meet people you haven't met before and they all want to know what you do for a living? It's so they can easily judge you and in turn judge themselves. People would change their behaviour based on your label and their perception of you. Imagine that you've arrived at an event where someone very famous and respected is speaking. You might approach the person serving the canapés differently than you would approach the keynote speaker because you have labelled them based on their role.

Sometimes you just need to break free from parents

Parents have functions to perform. These functions include protecting the kids, making sure they are getting what they need, participating in their development, and teaching them tradition and culture. After many years of performing these functions, it may be difficult for the parent to stop performing them. Even though the child has grown into an adult the parent wants to make certain that the child does everything the parent believes they need to do in order to be safe, happy, and healthy. The parent tries to control them, because they feel they know what is best for the child. They have spent all of their life controlling the child and cannot stop themselves from imposing on the adult child's life even when it is no longer appropriate. This is common when the parent has become too attached to the role of parent. Li Na was the child of parents who were trapped in the role and in return Li Na was trapped in the role of daughter. The people of both of these generations were products of their conditioning. They operated without thinking, without consciousness and purely out of habit.

Li Na is a young woman who wanted to break free from the tradition, buy a condo, and move out. She had stayed in the family home because in her culture, women don't move out of the parents' home until they are married and if they didn't marry they stayed at home with the parents. Li Na's parents continued to make decisions for her and even at the age 30, Li Na had a curfew and had to obey the rules the parents imposed upon her. Li Na believed that she was not ready or able to make decisions on her own. She had been conditioned to believe that she did not know enough about life or enough about Li Na to be able to make sound decisions for her own life.

When she began looking for a condo to buy for herself she did not tell parents because she was afraid of what they would say. She believed they would criticize her choice or tell her she had done it all wrong. She was afraid they would ask why she did it and why she had done it wrong. Had she clearly envisioned her own goal she would have become confident enough to reply that she did what was perfect for her. She would have realized that their perception of what was right for her was just that, their perception based on their own conditioned beliefs and it did not have to affect her own beliefs. Had she developed confidence in herself she would not have feared being judged.

Li Na dreamed that she wanted to buy a place of her own so she could have privacy and live by her own rules. Through conditioning she believed that her parents were the "Li Na experts", that they knew Li Na better than Li Na knew herself. I had felt that way when my mother told me I should get a job and marry my boss. I too believed that my mother knew me better than I knew myself at 17 years of age, and it took a lot to get me to see that this was not serving me well.

"Get this straight, *nobody* knows you
better than you know yourself. Your life
is about you and nobody else."

'Learn to live from the inside out, not the outside in

Get this straight, *nobody* knows you better than you know yourself. Your life is about you and nobody else. It's about how you are and not about how they are. How they are is their choice. Don't give your freedom away to mollify someone, make them happy or avoid making them angry or uncomfortable. These are privileges you should keep for yourself and never give away. What happens around you is not what happens inside you. Learn to live from the inside out, not the outside in.

There is a part of Li Na that didn't want to give her power away. It allowed her to entertain the thought of moving out but a deeper part of her belief system was that she not capable of doing it correctly. She was stuck in the role of daughter and the function of daughter was to allow the parents to control because they know best. To convince herself that she should branch out on her own and start living the life she wanted she believed she had to find their version of perfection to avoid being criticized for doing it wrong.

She was wise enough not to tell her parents because she recognized the need for a different support group, one that would encourage her bold move away from the traditional role of daughter of immigrant parents. Finding support would help her tap into her self-esteem and her own power. By beginning the process of searching for a home to buy she showed signs of knowing that she had some self-esteem and she demonstrated a desire to tap into her own power. Unfortunately, she did not hold on to the conviction that she could do it and in the end she gave up the home search and did not buy a home.

She told me that if she had informed her family their input would have proven too oppressive and would not give her space to think about what she wanted. She recognized the circumstance and yet she allowed it to stop her anyway and even though she had not involved the oppressors, she allowed them to stop her. Rather, she stopped herself, she sabotaged herself – she was the oppressor. Moving outside of your conditioning can be very difficult and tradition has created many habits including the habit of not thinking, and simply obeying. Li Na had not yet created the burning desire to buy her own condo and recognized that it would be easy to get pushed off track. She was still afraid to break out of the jail cell made up of false beliefs even though the door had been opened. She had opened the door by allowing herself to consider purchasing a home and leaving the family home thus challenging the belief that she must follow tradition and stay in her family home. She could see that the door was open but was hesitant to run out of the cell and into her freedom.

Li Na believed she was not good at making decisions, but I saw that she was very good at saying "no", which is a decision. The problem was that she had trouble with saying "yes". She was shutting out opportunity by saying no, she was limiting herself. She allowed small peculiar things in each condo to hold her back from saying yes even when her support group called her out on it, pointing out that she was not thinking rationally. It was her paradigm, her egoic mind that was holding her back by telling her not to take this scary dangerous step into the abyss. She struggled to determine what she wanted.

Li Na would have benefitted from writing out her wish list and really focusing on it. I'm not talking about the number of bedrooms she wanted, I'm talking about the life of freedom she craved. She could have asked herself how she would feel once she owned her own place. Imagine all of the feelings she may have experienced: pride, power, independence, and more. They could be feelings she had never experienced before because she had never allowed herself to crave, to desire.

If she had been able to clearly envision her life once she had achieved her goal she would have had an easier time when she embarked on the home buying journey. By having a clearly defined goal her mind would have been more open to the change that was required to achieve the result she wanted. She could have visited various places in the city opening her mind to the lifestyle each neighbourhood offered. She would have found areas that had cute cafés, favourite shops and could have made friends there. She would have found it easier to envision herself there as a homeowner, an independent woman living by her own rules. She could have written out her goal using a specific date to achieve the goal. In Napoleon Hill's book *Think and Grow Rich*, there are many suggestions on how to create the goal, how to commit to the goal, and how to achieve it. I believe that if she had truly envisioned the goal and had taken the steps required to achieve a goal she would not have squashed her desires and tucked them into a little dark corner where they would collect dust.

Figuring out your deepest wants is not an easy thing to do. You get blindsided by your false beliefs, your conditioning. You may believe you don't deserve it, you are not worthy. You may believe that your father knows best, or like Li Na you may believe that you are not capable of making decisions. I knew that Li Na could make decisions, but she didn't believe it. She was so anchored to the role of daughter that she could not swim free.

Deep down she knew she had the power to do it and to do it right. But she didn't allow herself to hold on to the conviction that she could do it, that she would do it. Had she made a vision board or even if she had it in her head of how she would feel when she had this condo, in this neighbourhood by this date she would have been successful. Instead, she was focusing on the idea that she could not make decisions. By focusing on the negative she could not create the positive. By focusing on what she didn't want, judgment, she could not achieve her goal.

Know you can definitely do and have whatever you truly want. Live from the inside out.

The push we need

Alannah was in her late 30s and had been renting for 20 years. When she calculated how much money she had spent over the years renting apartments she knew it was time to move. When I met Alannah she had already been looking for a condo to buy for the past year or more and had seen almost 50 places. Right there I knew what the problem was. It was not that the real estate did not suit Alannah, it was that Alannah was not ready to see the opportunity that was all around her.

She had lived in her apartment for so long her rent was way below market and that concerned me. I advised her that she would be spending more money every month in order to purchase. I was waiting for push back, but Alannah was aware that it would take more money but in the end she'd be ahead. She would own property and that would provide her with options in future and it would be a source of wealth for her.

She could own it outright in less than 20 years. She assured me she was ready to take on the extra costs associated with home ownership.

People who have a sweet deal on rent, who have great space in a prime neighbourhood may feel like they are taking a big step backward when they consider buying a home. They feel that way because they would have to give up space and location in order to buy within their financial means and on top of that they would have to fork out more cash each month! Those facts are true, and they can let it stop them if they wish. I've seen it happen many times.

Know what you really want and why

To overcome these issues you would have to really want to own your home, and you must have a clear goal. If you really want something you will not mind making the small sacrifices needed to achieve your dream. When someone comes into my office for a buyer consultation I advise them that buying real estate in Toronto is not for the weak of heart. On the road to success there are many obstacles.

> "When you choose your support group ask yourself if their beliefs are aligned with yours. Do they believe you should and could buy a home?"

Alannah gave the signals that she was ready to buy a home. Smart move on her part, she brought in the heavy hitters as supporters. She knew her friend would push her and her brother was sick and tired of hearing her excuses and would call her out on her nonsense when needed. She added me into the mix, and we were grooving. When you choose your support group ask yourself if their beliefs are aligned with yours. Do they believe you should and could buy a home? You will find this very valuable when you begin to flounder in your sea of fears and rationalizations as these people will keep you aligned with your goal. If your friend is negative she will reinforce your fears and hold you back.

You should observe the people you hang out with on a regular basis. Ask yourself, are they generally positive people or are they always complaining, whining and have a Debbie Downer outlook on everything. If you want to change your beliefs you will have to distance yourself from the negative energy. You can socialize on a superficial level with those people but when you are struggling with your own positivity you should know that you have the option to say "No, I don't want to see you right now." Find people who share your beliefs and will support your goals. If you can't find anyone don't worry. You are your own best friend. You can give yourself the help you need by simply determining what it is you really want, knowing why you want it, setting the positive goal, adding the plan, and acting on it immediately.

Create an affirmation

Create an affirmation that clearly states who you are once you have achieved your goal and how you feel. The best way to boost your faith in yourself is to repeat it aloud, write it out, visualize it, listen to it on a recording many times each day. Done and done! If you don't believe me, just try it out and mark what happens within a month or two of concerted effort. Keep a journal, write down any inspiration that comes to you and review it after a month. Notice the changes in your attitude, notice the negative ideas that used to come into your consciousness and how they've been replaced with thoughts and energy that serve you well.

Alannah and her support group saw some great places and some not-so-great places but this journey was less about real estate than it was about Alannah's habit of self-sabotage and fear. When we found a place that surpassed her expectations, Alannah started to pull back using the money as an avoidance technique. This was her fear rearing its ugly head. It was her egoic mind yelling, "Danger, danger!" Calmly, with no pressure, I asked her to tell me all of the thoughts that were coming up and stopping her from moving forward to her new life. "Let's analyze them to see if there is merit to them."

I suspected correctly that they were all rationalizations that she was using so she could justify backing out. I asked her to remind me of the reasons why she needed to move. She did this, one by one calling up the memories of the decisions that she had made while she had been calm. Then we reviewed the key points in the financial discussion we had had at the beginning of this journey together. She had already decided that paying more each month was a sacrifice she was willing to make in order to get what she wanted and to get ahead in life. Finally, Alannah allowed her love of the suite and her self-love to come forward strongly enough to win over fear. That was a huge personal success for Alannah.

Visualize your new life

The decisions Alannah had made while calm and serene were reflective of her true self. Those decisions helped her overcome the problems she would face throughout the home buying process. She was able to see what she wanted and acknowledged that they were good solid decisions that would help her move forward in her life and toward her goal of home ownership. These decisions had been coupled with positive emotions. She had been able to visualize herself in her new life, in a vibrant condominium complex, in a fabulous location with shops and restaurants she loved. She saw herself hosting her friends and family in her new home and feeling the pride and sense of accomplishment that came with the realization of a worthy goal.

Without those positive emotions and the work Alannah had done to help her break her habit of self-sabotage she would still be a renter today. It's just that simple; believe what I'm saying. The journey was not about buying real estate it was about overcoming fear and about knowing what she wanted. Alannah will be able to draw on this success for the rest of her life and create anything she wants. She has experience with overcoming objections and self-sabotage and can use this experience to set the tone for the rest of her life.

Decision, having made one or not, makes a big difference in what you will achieve. Everyone has experienced periods when they have struggled to make a decision, having mixed feelings about what to do or not do. Your egoic mind has one function, to keep you safe. Whenever something is new, does not follow the pattern of what you know and have been doing all of your life, or you've never seen it done before, or have never allowed yourself to dream about it your ego stops you. It's really imaginative in how it does it. It tricks you. You believe that your mind is thinking but it's not. The ego pushes your false beliefs to the forefront, reminding you it's the way it has always been done. Your ego doesn't want you to change or to try something new.

Changing your ego's story takes work

Think about tradition and *The Lottery* by Shirley Jackson. We blindly follow tradition even when it no longer has relevance and even when an outsider would find it absurd. We cannot see the absurdity in the situation because our ego will not allow us to see it in full light. It wants us to see the false version it has created for us. As a result, we dare not try to change it. Remember they would not even fix the old black ballot box for fear of some ramification they could not even imagine. The old man thought that giving up the lottery would cause them to revert to living in caves. The story allows us to be observers and to be objective. That allows us to see the truth clearly and even though you may scoff at the story and say it would never happen, the truth is that we allow ourselves to live that way, to live with the false stories that our ego tells us and to believe them beyond a doubt. These are stories that have been shaped over the course of our lifetime and to change them takes work.

Remember Lily who hadn't decided whether she'd buy or rent was told to make a decision and then call me? I mentioned that I was saving her from failure that would then hold her back or cause problems for her later on. If she had started the process to buy a home without a clear vision or strong decision she would have backed out when the first obstacle arose. Let's say we had toured some homes together and she found one that was acceptable to her, one that was offer-worthy. Other buyers felt the same way and were preparing their offers at the same time. She and I would have looked at the comparable sales and would have discussed her offering price based on the statistics and the market conditions as well as many other factors.

It's quite likely that during the time we studied the comparable sales, her old paradigms would have come into play and she would suddenly begin to find a way out of buying the home. It's too small. We just started looking, and I haven't seen enough. I don't like this or that. Then, the big one would appear: I only want to pay this much for it. She would have reviewed and understood the comparable sales, she would have acknowledged that she would have one shot at it to win it, and then she would have picked a number that she knew was safe, a number that she knew would not be accepted by the Seller and would not win in competition. I mean, that's assuming that we had even made it that far in the process but my experience tells me that we never would have gotten there. She would have found something wrong with every property.

While it could be true that some or even most of the properties were not appropriate, the reality is that her ego would have made up some story about why she should not buy any property. The ego would be screaming "Danger!" and she would react to that false belief by sabotaging herself. She would do this until she was priced out of the market or had become so frustrated that she decided to put a hold on things for a while. In other words, she would have failed, and then she would have been terrified to fail again so she would never try. She may have gone through the rest of her life without hope and what a horrible life that would be. That would make it even more difficult to overcome the ego and take the necessary steps to win.

It's one thing to give it your all and then lose. That's not failing. Failing is when you allow your fears or other negativity to take over and control your actions, causing you to give up.

When someone says they want a three-bedroom two-storey house in a certain neighbourhood and their affordability is 'X' dollars, they really believe they will buy it if it becomes available for sale. There are some people who will be overjoyed when it becomes available and there are others who will react like a cornered rat. Holy cow, Sandra pulled a rabbit out of a hat and now I have to deal with it! Shit's getting real! I see it happen in this business and it's something else to watch. The fear can come out at any stage of the race. It can stop you from getting started, it can stop you midway, it can even stop you one centimetre from the finish line. Buyer's remorse is fear that pops up after you've won the race. Get a grip on the fear, on all of the false beliefs you have. Don't sabotage yourself. Make the decision to get what you want.

If you suffer from low self-esteem you will find it difficult to make a decision. A person who is confident will make decisions easily and is not afraid to make a mistake. If they make a mistake they'll change it, they will fix it or abandon it and learn from it but they won't let it bring their self-esteem down. A mistake does not challenge their self-worth, they are too confident for that to happen. They know they are worthy, and they go through life without the frustration of indecision. Indecision comes from poor self-esteem and it will stop you dead in your tracks. Working on your self-esteem might be a good place for you to start. Enhance your self-image by becoming aware of the false beliefs you hold on to.

CHAPTER 10

Stop Being a Victim

"I've had thousands of problems, most of
which never actually happened."
—Mark Twain

I worked with a lovely woman, quite spiritual, had experienced some pretty daunting issues in her life and had worked toward resolving them, gaining financial security and a good life.

She called me to help her find the right home for her. She had rushed and had purchased a quaint log cabin in the country, had renovated it and once she moved in she realized that she didn't want to live there.

She gave me a brief outline of her story, the life she lived as a child of parents with substance abuse, and later in the system as foster kids. She decided at an early age to go to university and worked toward that goal, succeeded and enjoyed a good career. She had overcome alcohol dependency, cancer twice, and was now thriving. It was so heartwarming to hear her story of triumph, how she had overcome obstacles and had lived her dream. She knew how to manifest, how to set a goal and achieve it!

What you think about becomes reality

One day in the car while we were driving to see houses, she admitted that she had the fear that she would lose everything and end up homeless. This really surprised me because my impression of her had been that she was in a positive mindset and had conquered fear. We talked about it a bit, and I suggested that she should focus on something much more positive, in fact the opposite of the scenario she had just mentioned. Worry is a very strong emotion and what you think about becomes reality. Your belief determines your actions so it's super important to dominate your thoughts with what you want and with positivity. We manifest our reality. Your subconscious mind does not differentiate between negative and positive. With an emotion as strong as worry you essentially give the order and it will be carried out. Be aware of this, be conscious to give the right orders and they will be carried out. She understood what I meant by that and knew it to be true from the years of work she had done on herself and the knowledge she had gained by reading and through her own experiences.

"We manifest our reality. Your subconscious mind does not differentiate between negative and positive."

We had worked together, as a team, and it was going along very well. As an objective observer, I was able to keep her true to her wish list. When she started to feel pressure because time was ticking she began to consider properties that were not much better than where she was already. I talked her out of several properties that did not meet her true wish list. Soon, she found a house she liked, we showed it to her brother, and he liked it too. We talked about the pros and cons of the specific property because I like to tell my clients the full picture, good and bad, so that they can make an informed choice. They heard me out and she made the conscious decision to buy it. I drew up the papers, she signed, and the ball was rolling.

The listing agent told me he'd get back to me the next day, and on the following morning I received a counter offer. The Sellers had declined our offer and had made their offer to us. I called my client to tell her the news and to explain all of her options but before I could she told me she didn't want the house. Overnight she had fallen out of conscious decision and into automatic fear response. She had already talked herself out of buying the house. The excuses she gave me were the same things we had talked about and debunked the day before. Although we had already discussed the issues with the property they may have been a little over exuberant at the time and saw the light the next day. It was not a big deal, she had slept on it and were turned off the property. Onward and upward.

After a few weeks of looking we found another lovely house, and she was ecstatic. I was happy too, because the house worked very well with her wish list, and it was beautiful. After negotiations the offer was accepted. We went up a few days later to the house to have the home inspection but before entering the house she let me know the deal was dead. The reason was that her brother suspected there was toxic drywall in the house. There was a type of drywall that had been used during a housing boom that had proven to be toxic. I was familiar with the issue and I knew that it was something that could be remedied if it turned out that the drywall was toxic.

As it was only a suspicion that the drywall was an issue, I suggested that we continue with the inspection to determine if the rest of the house was sound. Instead of an inspector, she had hired a contractor who was going to renovate the house once she owned it. He was not familiar with the type of drywall we were concerned about so he did not offer an opinion.

I suggested at that point that we should hire an expert to come to the house to inspect the issues and to weigh in on them. My client was furious with me. She felt that I was pushing her and disrespecting her wish to back out of the deal. I was a little thrown off by this because she had loved the house, and thought we were simply assuming that there were issues but had not proven one way or the other. My job is to recommend the services of an expert to identify whether or not there is in fact a problem. In the case where there is a problem we could ask the Seller to remedy, ask for an abatement in price to cover the cost of the Buyer fixing it themselves or they could walk away from the deal at that time without penalty. If the an expert declared that there was no issue, the Buyer could proceed with confidence and complete the purchase of their dream home. By stripping away the layers of uncertainty we could see exactly what we were dealing with.

I asked if she wanted to have an expert inspect the property in the coming days. She did not answer me and was very upset with me when we left the property. I knew that she would need some time to calm down before I could speak with her on a rational level to pursue an appropriate tactic to address the suspected issues. At that point, I relayed the information to the listing agent who in turn did what was right for her client and brought in the appropriate expert the next morning. The expert certified that the gypsum or drywall was perfectly fine and was not the toxic type they had feared, and that the house had been built prior to the time frame that the defective product had been used.

My client was adamant that the expert had lied. She was beside herself that he had even put his stamp on the letter. My client could not accept the evidence. Her paradigm caused her to change the evidence instead of her false belief. She had the deep-rooted habit of fear that I did not expect to come up. This woman had been a champion, had overcome cancer not once but twice. She had overcome the obstacle of poverty and attended university gaining a degree, she had achieved success in her career and had overcome substance abuse. She had been tried so many times and each time she had won. It was shocking that she would freak out at buying a house, which seemed so miniscule in light of all that she had overcome. But it wasn't shocking really.

The belief that was causing the behaviour was the belief that she was a victim. It was her habit and she would unconsciously create circumstances to validate her role as a victim, time after time. Victims are not accountable for their own lives, they blame the circumstance, or another person, a perpetrator. A victim changes the evidence to fit the story they are telling themselves. She would not believe the expert was actually telling the truth. She chose to believe that he was sticking it to her. It was easier for her to believe that people were trying to cheat her rather than to believe that she was being dishonest with herself. If she truly believed the expert had ulterior motives she could have asked her friend in the field prove it. But she didn't let him inspect because then she might have to deal with evidence that did not support her role as victim. A victim plays "poor me" and sets themselves up to get hurt and to fail.

Victims blame circumstance by saying it's not fair, I don't know how, it's too hard, it takes money to make money. They blame someone else by saying they did this to me, I always get the short end of the stick, they don't get me. They fail to take control of their own lives, to take their own power by saying I don't have a choice, I'm tired, I can't, help me.

She went from a champion who had overcome so many bad circumstances to a victim in a heartbeat. This was most likely because of some self-doubt that she had allowed back into her belief system. It's possible that this happened after she purchased a property that she didn't like. She blamed someone else for the mistake and allowed doubt to creep in. She started to doubt her ability to buy the right home and allowed certain triggers to make her freak out. Because her self-esteem was not resonating high enough she allowed the mistake to throw her off, unlike a confident person who would learn from it and then change it. Instead of learning from it and then moving on she allowed the doubt to cause behaviour that did not serve her well.

"It's important to work on yourself every single day for the rest of your life."

Create daily rituals that help you stay positive

This proves that it's important to work on yourself every single day for the rest of your life. It's important to have worthy goals that encourage growth. Think of a beautiful garden that you weed every Saturday morning. You pull the weeds out to make sure the roots of the beautiful flowers can get enough nutrients and water in order to thrive. Think of your positive thoughts as the flowers and think of the negative ones as the weeds. When you miss a few weeks of tending your garden, you look out to see it's overrun with weeds and the only things thriving in your once beautiful garden are the weeds. The flowers have wilted and died as the weeds took over. It's just that easy. It took a lifetime to develop these negative habits and it will take a lifetime of positive thoughts to keep you on the path to living the authentic you. You can pull a weed only to come back the next day to find two more in its place. Think of the work of growing beyond your conditioning as lifelong. Create daily rituals that help you stay positive. Read, listen to or say beautiful enlightened thoughts, surround yourself with the right people and be positive, use positive language.

Victims are not really victims; they play the part of victim and in doing so they relinquish their power. Only when you take responsibility for your own life do you take your power back. By blaming others you become a prosecutor. By justifying your action and reaction and by complaining you take the role of victim. You may feel relieved by your justifications, but that is only temporary. Eventually the feeling of relief wears off and you are left with the truth that you did not achieve your dream, you did not succeed. You only fail once you quit. By failing you may never have the drive to try it again.

As Mark Twain's quote suggests, we often worry unnecessarily, and thus restrict our lives by some imagined drama. We often ask ourselves "What if?" and it can cause anxiety and fear. When you ask "What if . . ." the answer could be a bad thing or it could be good. What if the drywall is faulty? There are options: i) walk away ii) find out the cost of the remedy and see if the seller will accept a price abatement or iii) ask the seller to remedy. Or the answer to "What if the materials are faulty" turns out to be no, it is perfect and you can buy the dream home you fell in love with. You always have choice, and by choosing fear you are making a choice.

In the following pages, you will meet Sydney who did not accept defeat when her boyfriend kicked her out without her share of profit. She did not give up her hopes of homeownership when she lost her job. She didn't give up on the extensive amount of work that was required to make her house liveable. She chose strength, determination, and persistence. She could have blamed the circumstances and packed it in, lived with her mom. She was welcome there, it was an option, but she didn't ever allow herself to believe she was a victim. She took her power back and she kicked butt.

Find the key in awareness

When your egoic fear takes over it creates a story that is pretty convincing. You hear the story and you convince yourself that it is rational. You do not recognize it as conditioned response. Soon, you own the thought. You allow yourself to own the fear, to own the story. Then, the story owns you and you can't tell the difference between what is authentic and what is conditioned. When you are not aware of the conditioning you cannot change it. You can never be locked in once you are aware that there is a key to let you out. Change becomes possible once you find the key in awareness.

Stop the habit of worrying, of anxiety and fear. Do not allow yourself to be in denial, to play the victim, to blame circumstance or people. You create your own reality, so why not make it joyful, liberating, and limitless?

The Warrior: Know Yourself and How You Deal with Obstacles

Sydney is a single woman who shared her story with me in hopes that other women will take on home ownership for themselves. She believes it is the best way to build financial security, and believe me when I tell you, she knows what it's like to be without it.

She had been involved in a relationship with a man who bought a house and the two of them lived together in the house and renovated it. Sydney put her heart and soul into the house believing that the relationship was lifelong and that together they would build equity and roll it into a bigger, more expensive dream home. She was already handy and contributed to all of the work including dry walling, mudding, taping, tiling, and more, working nights and weekends, dedicating herself to the task and the goal of moving up.

Once the renovations were done, Sydney says that her boyfriend broke up with her and kicked her out. He sold the house and since her name was not on the title he didn't share the substantial profits with her. She found herself heartbroken, alone, and no longer able to live in the home she had renovated. She was angry, hurt, and felt used by him.

She suffered some downfalls in her career in a volatile industry and due to the nature of work, she was laid off three times within a short period. The setbacks were tough and emotionally difficult because she questioned her value and her self-worth. An optimist, she proceeded with the belief that the universe was nudging her in the right direction and that she would find something better. She continued to network

SANDRA RINOMATO

with people, building bridges. She became very proud of herself that she was able to overcome the challenges of the unforeseen changes in her career. She believes that how you face challenges is very telling, that knowing yourself is number one.

Sydney, a bit of a maverick and an outlier, wasn't like anyone in her family. This woman was a risk taker and embraced learning, new opportunity, and challenges. New jobs meant new skillsets, new people, knowledge, and expanding horizons.

She took her ex-cohabitator to court and won a small settlement that she promptly used to pay off student loans and put the rest into a home purchase. Her mom thought Sydney wasn't ready to buy her own home. Her mom is risk averse and didn't want to see her get in over her head and lose everything. Others told her the market was too high, she would overpay and lose money, the market is going to crash. She knew that everyone would have an opinion, and most often the opinion would be that they would have done it better, that she did it all wrong and that she should not do it at all. She knew about the great potential to make money in real estate ownership because she had seen it with her own eyes on the house that she had renovated with her ex. She was not afraid; she was simply excited and committed to making her own home lovely and profitable.

Just do it

Her realtor told her if she could find a place she could afford she should buy it. She encouraged her to get on the property ladder, to just do it.

Sydney wanted this, had made the decision to buy a home, had committed to it, and found the support she needed, her realtor. For Sydney, this was a no-brainer. She had no fear, she had enough confidence to know she could do it, and she was a decision maker. No challenge was too big for her.

Let's go back to Lily who left my office without making the decision to buy. Her motivation was simply to be on her own, which was already outside-the-box thinking for her. Her motivation was not to buy a home. You could say she was taking baby steps, playing small, which is totally fine, if you are fine with living a small life. For the average person, hassles and obstacles are good reasons to play small or not at all. A warrior like Sydney knows that life is full of obstacles, challenges and that they are part of life and part of success.

Sydney bought what she could afford. It was in a state of disrepair to the point that she could not live in it without improving it first. This was probably a house that we would term a "tear down" and the only other bidder on offer night was in fact a builder. Let's just say, it was a real fixer-upper. She stayed at her mom's house, went to her job in a distant part of the city each day, then straight to the house in the opposite end of the city after work until 11:00 PM, and then home to Mom's in the west end to sleep only to do it all again the following day. Other than plumbing and electrical for which a licensed professional is required she renovated the house by herself for six months until it was ready to move into. This woman was committed, she was focused, persistent, and she was hard working.

Her mom had heard her stories about renovating the previous house but didn't realize the extent of her skill and knowledge. Sydney knows that women are intimidated by renovations but wants us to know that it's not nearly as hard as it looks. It takes time, it means you are going to get dirty, and when you make a mistake you just do it over. Self-confidence abounds in this woman! She was not afraid to make a mistake, she would learn from it, rip it out, and do it again.

During the time she was a homeowner, she lost her job twice. I asked her how scary that was for her and how she dealt with it. She said that she called her agent and asked her for advice. The agent told her which improvements to focus on just in case she had to sell the house. So every day Sydney went out on interviews for jobs and then came home and renovated. Soon, she had a new job and could breathe easier. Sydney said it was important to stay optimistic, to know that you would find a job, and that the message was loud and clear that she was not on the right career path. She just had to hold the faith that the right job would be offered to her. She recognized that it wasn't going to just appear, that she had to work to make it happen, and that is why she reached out to her network and kept searching diligently for a new job in any industry that could be intriguing to her. Sure enough, she found herself in a totally different industry and has been enjoying it tremendously.

"Knowing yourself is number one, how you face a challenge is important. Being optimistic is important. You can get caught up in the negative, the naysayers, but don't believe it, push yourself forward. Just push forward, believe in yourself." —Sydney

---

She is very happy she took the opportunity to purchase when she did. The house is lovely now and has appreciated substantially in value, providing hundreds of thousands of dollars in equity.

Are you going to overcome your obstacles or are your obstacles going to overcome you? Anything you can't do or won't do is bigger than you. The challenges you don't deal with keep coming back and will keep getting tougher and bigger until you deal with them.

The practice of constantly overcoming challenges will force you to grow to a point where the challenge becomes easy. If you don't confront and overcome the obstacles what you are practising is being stopped by obstacles. You are conditioning yourself, either to succeed or to fail.

Let's look at the negativity people spewed when Sydney announced she would buy a house, because you'll find that negativity is more prevalent around you than positive thinking is. And that is not just about buying real estate, it's in every aspect of life. You know, they say misery loves company. I understand that to mean that people who are miserable in their little lives love it when someone else is miserable as well. Deep down they recognize that they could have lived bigger lives, they could have taken risk, overcome obstacles and could have done a lot of things differently. In turn, they don't want to see you succeed. It challenges their ego if you achieve as much as or more than they have. Remember that people want to judge you and themselves, and they want to compete with you and therefore create labels. They feel threatened by the success that an average person achieves. They want to believe that the rich get richer, it takes money to make money, and that only people who are born with silver spoons in their mouths will ever be rich. They believe that the rest of us are doomed to mediocrity. They justify their own mediocrity and either knowingly or unknowingly try to keep you down.

When my friend Rick announced his early retirement, people at work did not congratulate him, ask how he was able to achieve such an early retirement, and marvel at the wonderful life he had created for himself. They were not overjoyed for his success and excited about his journey and some people who had previously been friendly stopped talking to him altogether. Don't kid yourself, if you were to win a big lottery today the people close to you would despise that fact and would be angry that you had won and they hadn't. I saw that exact scenario happen to someone close to me so you can bet your bottom dollar it happens.

It's them not you

When I landed the job on *Property Virgins*, I met a guy we nicknamed The Host Whisperer. Peter Joseph had been sent by the network to help me become a TV host. Up until this point, I had never hosted a television series and had been working away as a realtor. After filming me for 10 minutes on camera he shut down the camera and said, "Don't change a thing." That was the end of the session thankfully because I had no acting skills and had already turned down the job so many times that if I hadn't been so comfortable on camera I'm certain I would have quit! He sat down in my living room with my little Netherland Dwarf bunny named Dutchy in his big hands and fell in love with her. He said to go ahead and talk about whatever I wanted to so I asked him what I could expect going forward. I had a new career in television and had no idea what to expect. I hadn't longed for or wanted a television career so I had no understanding of what was going to happen.

He thought about it a while and he said, "Well, people around you, and I mean close people, friends and family, will change. They'll say it was you who changed but it's them. Your success will make them feel insecure about themselves, and they will change." To be honest, I had already witnessed a bit of this phenomenon when I became successful in real estate but I had been unable to identify what it was or why it had happened. The premiere of *Property Virgins* was in October of 2006, and the show was extremely successful right away.

I went to a Christmas party at a friend's house in December and saw exactly what the Host Whisperer had foretold. I saw many people whom I'd known for years. One of them, my friend's cousin, came to me and for no reason and for the first time started talking about his wealth. He assured me that he was quite comfortable financially and didn't need to work. He said he didn't have a mortgage. He went on and on about this. It was almost like it had been set up. I was expecting Joseph to show up and say, "Ha ha – gotcha!" but he never did. This was real. I had known this guy since I was 16 years old and we had never discussed our financial situations prior to this night. He was threatened by the new label he was using to categorize me: successful television host.

A woman I had considered to be a friend, smart, funny, and an achiever lashed out at me in a very long and very mean-spirited email that aimed below the belt. By this point in my life, I could not bear children because I had been diagnosed with secondary pulmonary hypertension and the medication that was quite possibly keeping me alive would cause deformity in the fetus. Besides that, my heart would probably conk out, and I would die. Pregnancy was not in the stars for me and I had accepted that.

She wrote some of the meanest things you can imagine, attacking me for not having children and boasting about her children in order to rub salt in the wound. She said some things that would have destroyed someone who was not secure in themselves, and who hadn't been prepared with some understanding of what was really going on behind the comments. I had been prepared by The Host Whisperer and my previous life experiences. She liked it better when she perceived that I wasn't successful. She didn't feel threatened by me when she felt that I was less successful than she was. Her feelings of superiority were being challenged by the TV show and she was reacting from that paradigm. Upon retelling the story someone said to me, "Well then, what you are missing

is the idea of a friend but you didn't really have a friend to begin with."
Wise words.

When you are secure in yourself and have a very strong desire to
achieve a goal you will find that you simply gravitate to people who
believe in your vision and one way or another, by your choice or theirs,
you create a gap between yourself and the negative people in your life.
Your confidence and desire become so strong that these characteristics
act as a shield that causes negative comments to bounce off of you. If
you find that you are easily dissuaded, you should revisit your WHY list
and develop a stronger desire and by doing so you will find the confidence to help you achieve success.

CHAPTER 12

Perfectionism: Fearing That if You Fail, Others Will Think Less of You

I was working with a woman named Colleen who had decided to pur-chase a condo on her own. She had been renting an apartment for years, and the rent had stayed very low. Her apartment was in an was older building so there weren't many fabulously enticing features or ameni-ties such as you would see in a modern condominium, but the space was large, functional, and comfortable. Colleen expressed some concern about leaving her large space for a smaller space as she recognized that her current living area was much larger than she could hope to pur-chase. However, it seemed like she had come to terms with that and had determined that she was going to purchase. She had saved up a substantial amount of money for a down payment over the years and felt she was ready to do this.

I began working with her in January and very soon after she offered on a loft that had been on the market during the previous few months and had failed to sell. Unfortunately, it seemed that all of a sudden, many buyers had woken up with the idea of purchasing a loft, had offered on this previously unsellable property. The price it fetched was substantially higher than historical data would support and higher than Colleen wanted to pay.

Based on the current market conditions, we acknowledged that it would be costly for her to buy a trendy loft with 18-foot ceilings and floor to ceiling windows and because Colleen was unwilling to spend her top budget to buy a loft, we began to look at condo apartments with more determination. She wanted more than average square footage, wanted the extra space a den would offer just in case she decided to have a child in future, and she wanted it to be in a decent area with good access to public transit.

We looked for several weeks and although she did not become excited enough about a property to offer on one, we watched as the prices did something very extraordinary. I had worked in real estate in the area for over 20 years up to this point, and I knew from experience that condos in the area did not perform as well as downtown condos and in some cases the prices barely increased from one year to the next. I was surprised to see the prices of these condominium units increase almost weekly.

We would see a suite in a building sell for $380,000 and then within a week or even a few days, we'd see a similar suite, perhaps a floor lower or higher, with better or not as nice finishes sell for $385,000. This was something I had not witnessed in the resale condo market in the suburbs, and Colleen and I discussed this phenomenon at length. This was happening, it was real, and Colleen witnessed it with her own eyes.

I began my career in real estate in 1996 following a recession of the late '80s, just as the real estate market caught on fire and became the topic of choice for just about everyone, journalists included. The prices had fallen and in 1996 they began rising steadily. I saw the beginning of the concept of multiple offers and how it morphed into an entire process. The listing agent would begin by naming an offer date a week after the property was first advertised for sale on the MLS system in order to give people the opportunity to view the property and prepare their bids. Buyers would offer to pay more than the asking price and the procedure for both Seller and Buyer morphed into something akin to a private tender. I had often been a listing agent and also a buyer's agent and had sat on both sides of the table since the beginning of multiple offers. I quickly learned what it would take to win in these situations. I learned the little tricks that could cause the Seller to accept your offer over that of numerous others, even if you didn't offer the most money. I became very well-versed in the practise of multiple offers.

Colleen and I discussed the phenomenon at length. I would inform her of the selling prices of all of the suites we viewed together in person or on the MLS. We talked about the causes, the effect, and the dangers of it.

When a sudden and inexplicable jump in prices occurs, one of my fears as a realtor is that the appraisal for financing might come up short. This could happen due to the fact that at that time, the appraisers only used closed transactions for their comparative data. They would take data from the registry office using information on properties that had already been paid for and changed ownership. They would not take into account the sales that happened over the last several weeks or months as reported by the real estate board and had not yet changed hands. So while we watched prices go up and up with each passing week, the appraisers were still looking at data from a much slower and very different real estate market.

When the bank appraisal comes in light, the buyer may have to find extra funds to cover the shortfall. For example, if you paid $450,000 for a condo and the appraiser using outdated data found that the value of the suite was actually $430,000 the bank would only loan on the lower figure that the appraiser had provided. The buyer would have to come up with an extra $20,000 or so to cover the gap. It could be less than $20,000 depending on the lending ratio. If you are asking for a loan of 80 per cent of the value, you may only have to come up with 20 per cent of the shortfall, $16,000 in this case. A high ratio mortgage of 95 per cent would require an extra amount of $19,000 from the buyer.

Many times, this shortfall comes as a last minute surprise to purchasers and when they don't have deep pockets it can be very stressful and costly to borrow the extra cash. Failing to close on the property carries significant unpleasant consequences and should be avoided. A mortgage is a secured loan and the bank will advance money based on a calculation of a percentage of the value of the security, the real estate. The lenders determine what percentage they will loan based on your ability to service the debt.

I coached Colleen on this and we were well prepared for such an event should it occur. Colleen had saved up plenty of money and would be able to cover off any discrepancy without affecting her financially.

As a buyer, Colleen held on to certain beliefs and wish-list items and she didn't love the "bowling alley layout". Most of the affordable options offered the layout she didn't like and felt were too small. She also wanted it to be in excellent condition. She didn't want to spend almost a half a million dollars on something that she had to do work to. It became increasingly difficult for us to find a suite that she was happy with. She kept the idea of the loft she had offered on as a benchmark and would not reconcile the fact that a property like that was not attainable in the price range she had settled on. She had the ability to borrow more money and buy a more expensive property but she had determined the price that she was comfortable with. It hadn't really become an issue yet because we could not find another condo suite that she liked enough to offer on.

The buyer will determine the price

The prices were often set below value by Sellers and realtors in order to attract many offers. I have a problem with this way of doing things because it can make it more difficult for financing. It makes it very difficult for buyers to justify offering to pay $100,000 more than the asking price, if they haven't had the experience of watching the market and the prices increase rapidly. Colleen did have the experience and knew that we could not look at suites that were already priced at or above her maximum preferred price. It's a difficult situation for buyers and their realtors alike. It often takes one or two losses in multiple offers before a buyer can truly wrap her head around the fact that the asking price is merely a suggestion and the buyer will determine the price.

I see a lot of condos every week but when this one became available in a perfectly located building that was only a few years old, I was excited. I knew it was the one. This was a suite she could feel at home in. It was larger, had a spacious den and a great view. Best of all, it would probably sell within her budget, which meant this unit was within reach for her. Colleen felt the size was better than all of the others we had seen as it was about 100 square feet larger. That may not sound like much but it could be a 10 foot by 10 foot room. The balcony was very unusual, in a good way. It was completely isolated on the south side of the building with no other balconies around it. The suite was almost at the corner and there was no other balcony on the left. On the right, there were some balconies but they were quite a distance from this one and had a privacy wall that made this balcony feel very private. The southern exposure offered sunlight almost all day, and even had some views of the Toronto skyline and Lake Ontario. I was super excited about this one! I knew it was a gem and Colleen seemed to agree and was ready to offer on it.

We talked about price and while the offer process is private tender we could not know what other buyers were offering, we knew it would sell for more money than the smaller suites had been selling for. This was special, it offered everything Colleen wanted, and was available for purchase. We couldn't know for sure what the other offers were going to come in at, but I knew it was not the time to hold back a few bucks. I advised Colleen that she should give it all she had, not to hold back and to rest assured she would begin building equity from the day we wrote the offer. We had often discussed the offer process thoroughly and Colleen knew it would take a firm offer with no conditions on finance or Status Certificate in order to win. Offer day was a few days away. She had time to perform due diligence and to deliberate on her decision.

Colleen went back to her home and reached out to all of her support group. Somehow, during the time she left me and the time we spoke again she came to believe that she should not pay the $405,000 that we had discussed and she decided to hold back $10,000. Colleen offered $395,000. She based this decision on the fact that someone she had heard about had purchased a similar unit (although possibly not as large and more like the others Colleen had decided were too small) in the sister building the previous year. He paid less and Colleen could not reconcile the price that I believed would win the competition. I realize that it's a bitter pill to swallow but you must think about it in the proper perspective. You can start building profit right away, even before you move in. That equity would now start building for you too, and you would be able to make money on your investment. Besides, there's no use crying over spilt milk. You missed that opportunity. Let's focus on the one at hand.

Don't expect to pay last year's prices

I reminded Colleen that we had seen with our own eyes how the prices were escalating rapidly. I am sensitive to the fact that a realtor can sound like a pushy salesperson who is not concerned with the welfare of their client. I also know that this was a situation that warranted a reminder that regardless of what had transpired in the past, the present was what we had to be concerned with. Yes, this other person had gotten a sweet deal last year and had already earned tens of thousands of dollars in equity. Colleen had to be reminded to look at the empirical data that we had collected together, we had to be reminded of her own experiences and what we knew as the truth. Colleen could not expect to pay last year's prices, the price that was appropriate before the phenomenon of increased demand in the very price range, location and housing style that Colleen was hoping to buy.

Like I said, it's not easy for a buyer to swoop in and easily adapt to the idea of paying much more than the asking price. Colleen was not swooping in. This was months after we had begun the home buying process, months of rising prices and demand and a reduction of inventory to historical lows. The law of supply and demand was at work here and there was no way around it other than to find a home that wasn't as popular at the time. A two-bedroom condo was more expensive and was more readily available because fewer buyers could afford the price. The price range that Colleen was looking in had become the most in-demand of the year so far.

She started throwing out some resistance with issues that had never come up before. "Well, what if I have a baby?" I knew that she was reacting in fear but I took the time to address the excuses. She wasn't pregnant and she wasn't planning on having a child soon but she knew that one day she would. I reminded her that she had already thought about it and had decided that the den would provide the necessary space for a child and many would be grateful for the space at any age, and by then she'd have most likely built up some good value in the condo. She could sell the condo and roll the profit into a bigger place. At that time, she might have a partner and their combined income would allow for a more expensive property, even a house. She could be earning more money and could afford a more expensive home. Or, she could stay there, refinance and rely on the profit to carry her while she stayed at home to raise her child, or she could rent it out and live elsewhere. She had options. I was happy to hear she had dreams of motherhood in her future but it didn't have to mean that a future dream should hold her back from achieving her current goal. Tension happens when part of you wants to stay and the other part of you wants to go. Tension becomes fear.

She kept coming up with excuses, "My rental is bigger than this, and I'm comfortable in that neighbourhood because I have lived there for so long." I agree that she was about to take on a big debt and would have less space to show for it and would have to move to a new neighbourhood. These issues hadn't been problematic when she had been calm and rational but now her fears were causing her to find some reason to back out of buying her dream home. We had discussed them all and she herself had made the decision to pursue a home in the neighbourhood the condo was located in. She kept coming up with more objections that she had previously worked through.

It was more comfortable to stay in the rental because it did not challenge her. It also did not serve her dream and the money she would pay out in rent would be lost to her forever. She would have nothing to show for it, she would gain nothing financially. Sometimes renters initially feel that buying a condo is a step backward because they would pay more for less space, but after 10 years of homeownership they would have paid off a substantial portion of the mortgage, and more if they took advantage of pre-payment options. A portion of those monthly or bi-weekly payments will go toward paying off your principal loan as well as interest. In 10 years at 2.5 per cent on a $350,000 mortgage paid bi-weekly approximately $128,000 principal is paid off. If you continue to rent for 10 years and the landlord then sells the place or takes it over for herself you would have no option but to move somewhere else. The money you paid in rent is gone and is in someone's possession. If you need to or want to sell your condo after 10 years you will have earned equity by paying down your mortgage principal, in this case $128,000.

Even if the value of the condo suite had remained steady and had not increased you would still have your original down payment amount plus the equity built by paying off the mortgage loan. If the value of the property had increased you would have the profit, calculated as the original cost subtracted from the new sale price. Subject to adjustments and expenses, you would have access to your original down payment, your equity built by paying the mortgage down plus the increase in value and all of this is tax-free income from your principal residence in Canada.

Colleen was afraid. If one of Colleen's reasons for buying a home was to build wealth she would need to tap into her WHY and recommit to her goal in order to overcome the fear she was experiencing. No matter what the WHY is, the fear will always want to sabotage you, so stay connected to your WHY. Allow the all-consuming WHY to trample every fear.

An achiever thrives

Renting for 10 years prior allowed her to save money for the down payment, build up her credit, and prepare mentally for the challenge of buying a home. It served her well in that sense and now she would have to be determined to achieve her goal in order to beat down the paradigm that she was comfortable renting and should stay there. Staying comfortable does not encourage growth, does not allow you to achieve your dreams. Saying, "I'm fine renting, I'll get by" allows you to live a mediocre life at best. An achiever thrives and just getting by is not thriving.

> "When we can identify the belief that holds us back and causes us pain we can release it and move past it."

She was reacting like a cornered animal. Her egoic mind was sending her irrational thoughts as a last effort to stop her from breaking free from the status quo. She had made the decision to purchase real estate when she had been calm and at peace but now that the reality was before her she was frantically searching for a way out. Her mind was screaming "DANGER!" and she abandoned all rational thought and searched for excuses to justify quitting on her dream. When we can identify the belief that holds us back and causes us pain we can release it and move past it. We can become free of the controlling limiting thoughts. We can grow into our true selves.

Recommit to your goal each day

She had offered a lower price on the loft months previously but now that she had to spend a bit more money she was freaking out even though she had willingly increased the budget she had set for herself. She had become complacent in searching and never finding and now she had found what she had been looking for and suddenly became scared. The longer it takes to achieve the goal the less likely you are to remain committed to the dream. The way to combat that is to renew your commitment to the goal every single day. Use your affirmations to help with this, repeat your dream out loud, write it out, listen to a recording of it. Envision yourself after you have achieved your goal and feel the emotions around the reasons why you want this goal. Recommit to your goal each day. Don't allow irrational thoughts born of fear to control you.

Colleen didn't have enough faith in herself but she would have built that faith through repetition of her goal. You must trust in your ability to deal with whatever situations arise. You can never be sure of what the future will bring but you can be sure of yourself and sure of your ability to deal with it. With that attitude you never have to worry about what may never happen.

Worrying about something that may never happen is such a waste of time and energy. There is no use worrying about what may happen a few years down the road because you have no clue what will happen. By focusing on a potential disaster you will create the disaster because of the law of attraction and vibration. You will create the reality you think about and it's very important to be careful what you wish for. By worrying about something you will make it happen so put your energy into what you want and avoid focusing on what you don't want. Stop giving priority to the world you think and give priority to the world you desire.

Train yourself to speak in the positive

The ego speaks in the language of resistance and tries to avoid uncomfortable circumstances. It will tell you to be careful because you will lose money. If you believe what it says you will never gain money or achieve goals that are outside of your status quo. Colleen played to not lose money and it caused her the miss her opportunity to buy her home and to earn money on her investment. Her fear of suffering loss caused her to want to play small. Watch how rich people operate. They play to win, they do not play safe in order to not lose. It comes down to training yourself to speak in the positive and to abandon all beliefs that are created in fear. It comes down to believing in yourself and being able to make decisions from a position of power. Giving in to your fears robs you of your power.

Colleen talked it over with various people and decided that she would offer less than what she could easily offer within her own budget restrictions. She held back the $10,000 and lost it by $6,000. She had offered $395,000 and it sold for $401,000. If she had offered the full amount of the budget she had previously decided on while she had been calm, she would have won the deal by $4,000 and she would have benefitted from a 32 per cent increase in price in just 12 months' time.

Let me do the math for you. She would have paid $401,000 and after one year her principal residence would have appreciated in value to approximately $525,310 providing a profit of $124,310 tax-free dollars. Even if it had been a relatively slower year that followed her purchase and prices had only appreciated by 5 per cent, Colleen's home would have increased in value to $421,050 providing an increase of value of $20,050. If the value of her home had remained the same after one year she would have paid down a portion of her mortgage loan instead of paying the landlord's mortgage.

The profit, or equity, is tax free on your principal residence in Canada. You can make unlimited money on your home where you live and not pay a penny in income tax on the amount. Colleen continued to rent and did not purchase, which cost her money in rent. Let's say her rent was only $900 per month and she paid out $10,800 to the landlord in one year. Many would argue that her $900 payment was significantly less than her carrying costs on the condo, which would include principal and interest on the mortgage loan, property taxes, and maintenance fees. I argue that the $10,800 that she paid did not benefit her financially at all. She did not gain equity by paying down principal and interest, and she did not gain equity in property value appreciation. It may be possible that Colleen saved up more than $20,050 after-tax dollars and could be ahead if you calculate that the condo price had only increased by that much, but the truth is that the value of the condo she could have purchased had in fact increased much more than that, and there is very little chance that she would have been able to save up $124,310 after taxes. She did not earn enough money to do that.

It wasn't meant to be

Colleen is not the only person to make this mistake, and you could say, "it wasn't meant to be" which would be nonsense, as it clearly was meant to be and the $10,000 that Colleen held back cost her $124,310 in equity in one year in lost opportunity. She made the decision to hold back when it was irrational to do so. This wasn't a situation where she simply did not qualify for the loan or did not possess the funds to offer. It was not a situation where the price was not justified by statistical evidence that she had seen with her own eyes. Thus, it was meant to be, and she made a costly error. By using this excuse people give up their power to choose and fail to be accountable for their actions.

When Colleen left me on the day we had seen the condo she was excited and prepared to offer on the suite. After she went out to talk to her support group she must have come across some negativity, albeit unintentional.

Her dad was her protector and always took the role of being the wiser adviser. He was not a believer in condos in general and was unsure that his little girl should spend all of her hard-earned savings on a condo because he felt they were risky investments. Condominiums haven't been around that long really and for the first several decades, people in Toronto often said they would never buy one. I am familiar with this belief and I know it comes from lack of knowledge and is based on assumptions. Her dad most likely bought his house with his wife more than 30 years ago and never moved, raised a family there and lived happily ever after. He wasn't in tune with the reality of the Toronto real estate market. People had been buying and selling condos earning a fortune by doing so. He was not well-versed enough, not knowledgeable enough to advise her but his function as father was to advise and protect his daughter and he believed he was doing so by advising her to wait. We all play roles and his was the role of Dad.

Her dad had been following the media on Toronto real estate, which often seized any opportunity to instill fear in people's minds. He believed the market was on the verge of a crash and that Colleen would lose her money. He may not have expressed his fears, he may only have hesitated slightly or perhaps had a tone of voice, physical body language and negative energy that Colleen may have picked up on. She read the signs and learned to be afraid of the situation. She was stuck in the role of daughter and would not make a decision that went against her dad's advice.

The result was that Colleen wrote me a very long email detailing the conversations she had had with her sphere of influence and relayed information she had read in the newspaper and decided she would wait for the prices to crash and would buy when the prices were low. I was grateful that she had taken the time to write and saw it as a courtesy. I did not believe that the excuses she had written were the reason why she held herself back from purchasing the condo she loved. I hoped that she would come to see that her fears had held her back from succeeding so that she could identify and address those fears and move forward toward success in all aspects of her life.

Identify and address your fears – it's the only way to move forward

Colleen asked the people around her until she found the answer she was looking for, the answer that went against what she knew, and finally stopped searching once she had the support to sabotage her own goal because of fear. She ignored the fact that we had seen the prices go up, ignored the fact that she could comfortably afford home owner-ship, ignored the fact that tax-free equity was a real possibility for her and would increase her wealth and long-term financial well-being. She searched until she found someone who said no and ran with it.

Many people think themselves out of every good opportunity by over-thinking, over-analyzing, and spending too much time planning. They often wait for the perfect time, which never comes or has already passed them by. You've heard of analysis paralysis? I've watched so many women analyze their options so much that they became unable to make a decision. They became paralyzed and could not act. The more they search for certainty the more insecure they become.

Success conscious people make decisions quickly and confidently. They are not afraid to make decisions and are prepared to correct any mistake they do make. They do not allow the fear of making a mistake dictate their actions. They have enough confidence in themselves to know that they will be able to handle whatever comes their way.

"Success conscious people make decisions quickly and confidently."

Colleen was a perfectionist and perfectionists are afraid to make a mistake, afraid to be judged negatively. She was so afraid that even one person would be able to say "I told you so" that she stopped herself from making the decision that would have made her successful in her home purchase. She was worried about things that may never have come to pass. She was afraid that by failing, others would think less of her. Nobody knows for sure what is going to happen in the future and we make the choice to either take chances or to limit ourselves. Don't be afraid of making a mistake. The only people who don't make mistakes are the people who never try anything. People like to see others fail because it makes them feel better about their own failure. If you let it bother you, it would be because you are not confident enough in yourself. Find yourself and once you have a sense of who you are you will fly, soar above the mediocrity and fears that cripple so many others.

There is nothing good about perfectionism; it is crippling. It creates stress and anxiety, a fear of failure and a fear of judgment. Perfectionists have dozens of conditions around their success. Often they won't even start because they know it won't be perfect. A perfectionist will do something only if it's easy, comfortable, convenient, there is no risk, if they will look good to other people, and if everyone will like them. Those perfect conditions will hardly ever come together and because of that neither will your success. Colleen waited for the perfect place and then sabotaged her chance of attaining it. She created an obstacle by using a justification for offering less than it would sell for. She knew those prices were gone but she would not allow herself to accept it and purposely held herself back from finishing what she started. She would rather fail and stay within her comfort zone than to succeed in purchasing and allowing herself to enjoy the dream of home ownership.

Everything had to be perfect which is almost impossible and when everything was close to perfect she made something up. "The market is going to crash, my friend's brother paid less last year, the extra $10,000 is too expensive even though I've seen other stuff sell and I know it to be true pricing. I refuse to see the truth because my ego mind is yelling 'DANGER, DANGER'. Therefore, I make up a story so convincing I can even write it out for my realtor. I'll fool her!" Fool me or not, the fact remains that she failed. She lost the deal and then quit her home search and lost the opportunity.

She didn't want it badly enough, she didn't want it "no matter what it takes" because she had conditions. The conditions you set up are the only obstacles that are keeping you back from getting whatever you want.

Pay attention!

Client sees and likes a condo that is priced very low and is positioned for multiple offers. The price, which is merely a suggestion is $399,900. A similar suite sold eight days earlier in very similar condition and for all intents and purposes it was identical. The one that sold eight days ago sold for $480,000.

The client knows it won't sell for the asking price, he knows that one sold a few days ago for much more, in fact $80,000 more. He tells his agent he wants to buy it and states that he will offer $440,000.

The agent talks it over with his client, they discuss the recent sales until the realtor just can't say anymore and the buyer still believes that $440,000 is a great offer. Why? Why does he feel that way? The stats show him everything he needs to know about the current market value, the realtor explains to him they are identical units. Why would he think that $440,000 which is $40,000 lower than the one that sold last week, will get him this suite?

When the buyer loses and fails to win the deal he says, "It wasn't meant to be." Stop right there!

It was meant to be but you weren't paying attention. The danger in saying, "It wasn't meant to be" is that it allows you to forego any involvement, any responsibility, any accountability. No, it wasn't you, it was God. As if God didn't want you to have that suite! God/source/ Universe made you aware the property was for sale and gave you knowledge and information so that you could get it but you weren't listening! You were busy reinforcing your habit of being the victim. You were busy reinforcing your habit of failing to take responsibility.

Don't believe anything your mind says. It knows you and will attack your weak points, your hot buttons. It knows what you've fallen for in the past and just how to say it so you fall for it again. When you don't get the job done, deep down you feel like a loser, then you justify, and rationalize, and you shrink in spirit and confidence. That's why I get the long emails that are filled with propaganda from the people who back out. They are trying to convince me and themselves that they did the right thing. Those emails are filled with excuses and those excuses are never the real reason why.

Know exactly what you want and why

Your thoughts are the obstacles that hold you back. That's why you need to know exactly what you want, why you want it and what you are prepared to give up to get it.

By making a fresh commitment to your goal each day you will get rid of those nasty voices and you will replace them with the ones you choose for yourself. Observe the thoughts that come in to sabotage you. Just be an objective observer, hear the words that your mind is using on you. You'll notice that it's the same thing over and over again. Write them down and look at them. Write down what was going through your mind when you stopped yourself from taking action. You'll recognize a pattern and you'll see the same ones come up over and over again.

Take a separate piece of paper and write the exact opposite of what you have written down. For example, if your egoic mind told you that you were not smart enough to do it (it uses stronger language by the way) write, "I am confident enough and smart enough to do this." If you wrote that you don't deserve a better life write "I deserve the best life I can imagine and more." Write out the new statements believing that you have everything you need in order to achieve your goal and believe that you are limitless. You get the drill. You might even go so far as to burn the old list, make a ritual of it and be sure to doing it responsibly. Then keep the new list and review it as many times a day as you can. Memorize it and say it out loud as often as you can. Record your voice repeating these new beliefs and play it over and over again.

Do you want more excuses in your life or do you want results? Do you want to succeed or do you wish to fail? If you spend too much energy and time talking about it and you wait too long you won't take action on it. It's nice to have a dream, to have the desire to do something, to be committed to it but if you don't act on it simply becomes a nice little story you tell yourself.

This can work with any goal and I use this technique myself and with my agents for our business goals. Write out your reasons why you want the goal and each day write out the reasons why you didn't take the actions you know will get you closer to achieving your goal. It's a simple way to do what we are so bad at which is observing our own behaviour. When collected daily this data will be amazing for you. What went through your mind when the alarm clock went off and you hit snooze? What went through your mind when you were scheduled to make calls and you didn't?

You can use this technique for your home search too. When you found a great place to buy what stopped you, what thoughts went through your mind, what old script were you following, what old record was your mind playing? As you begin to overcome obstacles you will find the phraseology changes. That's because you already won the battle over the others, you found a way around the obstacle by removing it, by seeing it for what it really was. Nothing. Not real. Made up! Not a problem at all, just drama.

Find your WHY and write it out in detail. When you think about why you may phrase it in way that avoids pain, i.e. I want more money so I won't ever go hungry again. The negative language allows you to focus on being hungry. Shape the reason why in a positive light i.e. I want more money because I will feel good, have everything I want and will always have a stocked pantry. Allow yourself to dream as if nothing can stop you. Ask yourself what you would want if money was no object and if you had all the resources you needed at your fingertips. See the dream and feel it, commit to the goal, create a plan to get it take action immediately. Recommit to the goal many times each day. When obstacles appear review the list of reasons why you want this, recommit to the goal and overcome the objection. Achieve your goal, allow yourself to win.

Ciara's Time to Buy

Ciara wanted to buy a house in the suburbs. She was raised by a strong, smart, and independent single mother. Her mother worked two jobs because her dream, her desire was to get her children into a better neighbourhood. She was afraid of having her kids in an area that she identified as a bad neighbourhood, whatever the defining criteria was for her.

Her strong desire to protect her children and to give them as much of a head start in life as she could was driving her to work more, earn more, save more and earn the ability to get financing to own a home. Ciara witnessed this, she watched as her mother set a goal, as she attached emotion to it and then as she took action and achieved her dream goal. What a strong role model for this young daughter.

Ciara's mom didn't stop once she had achieved her goal. Once she had achieved the goal described above, she didn't sit back on her laurels and stop there. No way. She knew the benefits of being a homeowner and landlord so she set her sights on owning more property. There was no fear, she knew she could do it and because she wanted it she did it. Ciara's mom already owned multiple properties when Ciara and I met. She was a goal achiever.

Mom was an inspiration for Ciara and she saw that it was possible to achieve whatever you set your mind to. She had the attitude of "if she can do it so can I!" In this fact, Ciara had the head start she needed in order to lead a successful life. Earl Nightingale said, "Success is the progressive realization of a worthy ideal." In other words, success is moving towards achieving a goal. Ciara had the benefit of an excellent teacher who showed her the way to success by actually achieving it.

Once Ciara had set her goal of buying a house, and she knew she needed a little support to help her get there. She brought her mom along for the obvious reason that she had great experience and expertise in home buying and also because Ciara recognized in herself a potential habit that could cause her to make a bad decision. She understood that occasionally she would act spontaneously and she wanted her mom to help her keep that in check. Ciara recognized that her spontaneity could cause her to make a bad decision based on one superficial part of the house rather than carefully looking at the whole.

While it's essential to be able to make decisions quickly and firmly, Ciara understood herself well enough to know that she might make a faulty decision. Her mom knew that she would more than she could afford in the moment and that would not serve her well. She knew her role in the support group was to reel her in and to focus on the long-term investment in order to decide whether or not she needed the shiny object that had grabbed her attention. Ciara was aware that there were potential triggers that could cause this reaction and she was smart enough to find the solution before she got started. She decided to bring mom because she would call her out on this and wouldn't let her hide within the paradigm.

The other person in her support group who would tour houses with her was a friend. She chose this friend because she knew that they wanted her to get all the things she had dreamed of. They had watched her work hard to get to this point and they felt she deserved it all. They represented the other side of the coin, the fun side. Although she knew it was rational to bring mom, she didn't see how bringing them into the support group might actually negate the good influence of her mother's advice and could give her the opportunity to sabotage her own dream. I am not suggesting that her friend was wrong, not at all, and I do believe that they supported her home buying desire. I am suggesting that by bringing the friend in Ciara was creating an escape route for herself. She had brought in support that would help her justify something irrational, set up a new obstacle in order to be able to stop herself just before the finish line. It was good that the friend was there because she would have the support she needed in order to look at the whole picture and support to get the fun stuff too, within reason. They knew she had worked hard, saved hard, she had earned it and deserved it.

The key was to define what Ciara really wanted. It is fair to say that Ciara wanted the financial benefits of homeownership that she had learned were possible and profitable from her mother, an excellent teacher on the subject. That is one of my strongest beliefs and one of the best reasons to own real estate in my opinion.

I showed Ciara a few houses and in each of them she found something she would not accept. She had a clear idea of what she wanted and did not want. She would not accept one house because of the colours the walls were painted. Another house did not have stainless steel appliances which she had put high on her own list of priorities. When you have too many conditions around your goal you sabotage yourself. Focus on the goal. Is the goal to have certain appliances or is the goal home ownership?

We looked at a house that had a large living room that she could use to entertain family and friends. She felt the room was not big enough. These issues had become a common theme in every house we looked at including a large 2500 square foot house that she felt was too small for this single woman. In my work I've noticed that often times when single women are looking at homes to buy they get hung up on aesthetics and they over estimate how much space they need in order to live the lifestyle they seek. I wanted to understand why this was, identify the cause, and learn how we could overcome it.

You could argue that buyers just want to get as much as they can for their dollar. The appliances and amount of space may represent the biggest bang for the buck. When Ciara's mother was challenging her she accused her mom of trying to limit her and hold her back when in truth her mom was keeping her focused on the goal of home ownership. That was Ciara's feeling of inferiority coming out. Where does that belief come from? It comes from competing with others.

You base your ideal on what others have because deep down you feel inferior. You feel inferior because you judge yourself against someone else. You compete, therefore you strive to beat them, to become superior. The opposite could be true as well when deep down you feel superior and are afraid that you might appear inferior and lose the impression of superiority. You feel bad about yourself because of some false story you have accepted about yourself. You have repeatedly told yourself this story because of your conditioning. You spend time trying to make yourself feel better about yourself all because of some false story you believe. In the mean time you run the risk of missing the opportunity to live the dream right now. Besides that, you just feel bad and nobody wants that.

Focus on what is available

When I was working on *Property Virgins*, after the cameras stopped rolling many participants, we call them virgins, would ask me what kind of house I lived in assuming that it must be huge and gorgeous. I assured them that I did not live in a huge house and that I actually lived in one of the smaller houses in my neighbourhood. I walked the talk. Some of these people did not end up buying a house because they were unwilling to seize the opportunity at hand. These virgins wanted it all and they wanted it right now. They were competing and in the end they sabotaged their own dreams. My message was to focus on what was available to them right now that would allow them to continue on to the next stage of their lives. They could achieve the dream of home ownership right now, own a home where they could be happy, move forward to the next phase in their lives and then if they had the desire to move later in life they could dream and achieve whatever they wanted at that time.

Believe this: you are not inferior, you are not superior, you are simply you. You are one of a kind, nobody is like you, you are not like anyone else because we are all unique. There is no need to compete. Competition brings feelings of inadequacy and causes behaviour that is ultimately self-defeating. Stop competing. Be authentically you. You are amazing, you are limitless. If you can get into that mindset you won't be held back by erroneous beliefs and you will achieve your dream, your goal, and self-realization.

Revisit your WHY

One activity you should do is to focus on the reasons why you want to buy a home. I asked you to write them down earlier in the book, and you could revisit them now to make sure they are still aligned with your goal. When you are going through the process of buying a home you should have this list top of mind. Review it every day, many times throughout the day. Write it out, carry it with you, post it to the mirror you use every day. Read it out loud, say it in your head, you can even record yourself saying it and listen to it often. If it doesn't resonate with you stop and think about what's going on in your mind. What is the resistance? Be still, reflect on it, and be totally honest with yourself. Write down the thoughts that come to mind. You may find a recurring theme as you did this day after day and you will begin to become aware of a false belief that does not serve you well.

Ciara longed for impressive appliances and other aesthetics that in the grand scheme of things proved unimportant when considering the investment value of owning real estate. She had allowed herself to compete with her mom and maybe other people and that caused her to spin out, throw up obstacles that were not really there and almost sabotage her dream. Her dream was to own her first house and to soon buy many more houses. The colour of paint, the type of appliance does not factor into a dream like that. Investment security, potential for growth, resale potential, structural integrity and more are the important factors when investing in real estate. Ciara's dream was not to buy her ultimate dream home at this time. It may be a future dream of hers and I believe it will be, with bowling alley and infinity pool and if that is what she wants I am confident that she will get it. I also know that it will take a few steps to get her there.

Her goal was to begin her life in real estate ownership, which will eventually lead to the dream home and financial freedom. If she had not been able to make a shift that allowed her to recognize opportunity she would have searched and searched for the elusive unicorn known as the perfect house which could have caused her to fail and to never get on the road to her dream home. She learned to be flexible and to recognize opportunity when it came along. In the end she did not feel like she had sacrificed her dream because she had been able to acknowledge that the dream was home ownership. By purchasing her first home she has put in place an important piece of the puzzle that represents her successful life.

Often times you envision something, work towards it and miss it because when the opportunity presents itself it doesn't look exactly how you had it in mind. I was a tomboy growing up and as such I loved watching car racing. As a matter of fact, when I was 20 years old I would have leapt at the opportunity to race cars but at that time women were not involved in racing so I limited my dream.

When I was a little girl of five years old, I was watching a race on TV with my dad and he exclaimed at the Italian guy racing that day. "Mario Andretti," he said, rolling the r's and pronouncing his name the way you would hear in Italy. I remember that moment clearly. I've known Mario

Andretti's name since I was a small kid and have watched him win one championship after another and become the icon he is.

Fast forward many years to when my friend took me to a lapping day. A lapping day is where you rent a racetrack and take your cars on the track, often with an instructor. It's pretty cool and I was very excited. When I came off the track after taking eight laps in his Corvette I was drenched in sweat, my hands were shaking, and I was on an incredible high. One day I was retelling the story to my friend Heather and exclaimed, "If I could be on a race track at the same time as Mario Andretti for just two laps you could open the car door and shoot me dead and I would die a happy woman." I'm pretty sure she was disturbed by my announcement and could not believe her ears. Heather saw the passion in me, didn't relate to it and totally dismissed me. Less than two years later Heather took a job in the Indy Car industry at a time when Mario Andretti was the coach for his son Michael on Team Newman Haas. One thing led to another, and I ended up in a pace car with Mario Andretti before the Toronto race. They don't do pace car rides any longer and I think this may have been the last year they did it. A pace car would take you around the track for two laps. You see, I had somehow achieved my dream of being on the racetrack with Mario Andretti for exactly two laps.

Create a vision

When I had envisioned this happening, I saw myself in an Indy car and Mario was in his own Indy car and I was most likely nowhere near him because he's an icon and I'm not. What happened was even better! I was in the car with him! The passion with which I had declared my dream, saying it out loud to Heather at risk of being locked up, ended up manifesting my dream. I manifested my dream in a way that was even better than what I had imagined. So much had to happen to get me there that there is no way I could have orchestrated it if I had tried. I could have written a letter asking to meet Mario Andretti and get into an Indy car at the same time as he was on the track and I'm very confident it would not have happened that way. Instead, by saying it out loud, many times, to many people and to myself with an incredible amount of passion, I made it happen. I never believed it would happen and said it almost as a joke, without resistance, yet the passion and frequency with which I had said it created it.

Back to Ciara and her appliances, do you think that anyone would like Ciara better if she had stainless steel appliances? Do you think I would like you more, or perhaps less once I had seen your appliances? Do you believe that I would scorn you for having older appliances, white appliances or mismatched appliances? Why would anyone allow appliances to define who they are? What is lacking in them that they feel they must have the avant garde appliances to make them lovable or happy? Like Ciara, you may think having stainless appliances would make you happy, and they might but holding firm to the ideal could prevent you from purchasing a home altogether and that would make you very sad. Think about the pride of owning a home you have purchased with your money and you are paying for with your money. You make a home there, you are safe there, you bring family there, you are building financing security there. Will you allow yourself to be defined by your appliances or will you tap into your power and love that you are living your true self? The sense of accomplishment you gain when you achieve any goal feeds your soul and your mind.

How can you train yourself to live authentically? Frankly put, you have to not give a shit about what other people are doing or saying about you. You ignore your egoic mind that tells you to follow the norm. There is no norm. There are seven billion people on earth and no two are alike so what would you consider the norm to be?

A daily exercise for the rest of your life

Try this exercise. Grab a notepad and pen, calm your mind and your body, and sit quietly, eyes open or closed, as you wish. If your eyes are open try to focus on one spot. A lit candle works well here as does a spot on the wall across from you. Do some deep breathing, in and out while you think of five things you are grateful for. Feel the gratitude in your whole body. You have a lot more than five things to be grateful for, everyone does. If you don't think so, change your thinking. Start by being grateful for the breath you just took. It gives you life, it nourishes your body. Keep breathing deeply, taking long, slow, but comfortable breaths and envision the gifts in your life. Take your time, revel in the feeling of gratitude. By now you may sense your body vibrating, you will be very relaxed, you may even be weeping, or smiling or both at the same time. Do this at least once each day for the rest of your life.

"Gratitude is one of the most powerful human emotions. Once expressed, it changes attitude, brightens outlook, and broadens our perspective." —Germany Kent

---

Now, start thinking of all the things you want. This is harder than it sounds if you've never gone through this exercise. Make a laundry list of all the things you want, it doesn't matter how big or how small, and I encourage you to go big. A new car, a bigger house, a better job, a new career, your own business. Go on, dream, write everything down, do not allow your egoic mind to keep you from writing it down. It's busy trying to tell you can't have the things on the list but please ignore it. Get intense about your list, go wild, don't hold back. You will never have to show this list to anyone, it's just for you. Do this exercise several times until you get the hang of it. It took me months to be able to nail it so don't get frustrated if it doesn't happen the very first time you try it. As you practise you will notice that one or two items on the list really draw you to them.

Look at those things and ask yourself why you want them only to be certain that the list is truly reflective of what you really want and not what someone else wants for you. As soon as you are able to focus on one item that really inspires you, one that you want more than any of the others get a new page. At the top of a new page start dreaming about how you will feel once you have achieved or acquired it. Really get into it. Think of the emotions you will feel. How will you look? Describe in detail where you are. Who is there with you? What time of day is it, what time of year is it? What do you see? What are you doing? Be specific, the more detailed this is the better. By now you should be feeling all kinds of beautiful emotions, write them down on your list. Take your time and keep writing until you are out of things to write.

Now that you have completed this step, you should congratulate yourself on defining your goal. It is time to add this to your gratitude list. I know, you haven't acquired it yet. Don't worry about that, just go with it. Give thanks for it, feel the gratitude and all the other emotions you wrote down.

That person you envisioned in your dream is you. That's your authentic self. That's the true version of you. You are limitless, you are serenely powerful, brave, open, positive, grateful, strong, beautiful inside and out.

Ciara had been very fortunate in that she had a role model who led the way for her. She showed her that this dream could be achieved by achieving the goal. Her mom had the desire to move her kids into the suburbs into a home she owned herself. She dreamed it, planned how to get there and then executed the plan. Many of us didn't have that type of role model and had to find the courage to lead the way ourselves. Others had watched people fail in achieving their dreams and then lay low, too afraid to try again lest they failed again. And others still never watched a member of their family purchase real estate and thus did not develop the belief that home ownership is an achievable and worthwhile goal. No matter what your situation is, the following will help you define why you want to buy real estate and will help you devise a plan to help you get it.

CHAPTER 13

Book it!

When I met Narissa, she explained that in her culture the norm for a woman is to go from her parents' house to her husband's house and that no woman had ever bought real estate on their own in her family or within her community. Since she had moved to Canada, Narissa had opened her mind to every possibility, broke through the traditions of her culture, decided she would not wait for her soul mate and set a goal to buy real estate on her own. She was successful and happy in her new country and home ownership was the next step she wanted to take. She felt that owning real estate would provide that sense of belonging and stability for her, and I couldn't agree more!

She was tired of paying someone else's mortgage and ready to own a home so that she could build her own wealth instead of her landlord's. Owning real estate would allow her to pay her mortgage loan down over the years and make her feel like she had accomplished the biggest financial goal in her life.

She set her goal of home ownership and then created a plan to save money for a down payment on a condo. Narissa wanted to save $20,000 and sacrificed collecting old books in order to save it. Old books were very important to her and she dreamed of putting her book collection on display in her new home. I was very excited to work with Narissa because I could see all that she had accomplished in her life and her strong determination.

We had a heartfelt discussion at the beginning of Narissa's home buying process and it became evident that her wish list was not aligned with the reality of what her budget could actually get her. This is because when she created the plan of what she would buy she had no knowledge of the real estate market conditions and did not realize that her budget was below the average price of a condo in Toronto. She could still afford to buy a place but she wasn't going to get a big beautiful place in a spectacular location.

Know what the dream is

I needed to find out what Narissa was willing to give up to make her dream come true. She had decided that she wanted a den or spare bedroom to display her books for easy access and this was a big item on her wish list. I showed her that it was possible to get all of the items on her wish list but to get it all she would have to look outside of her preferred area. I showed her some places outside of her immediate area of choice but the location did not appeal to her.

Within her preferred area, the price of real estate was higher so to be able to afford a condo she would have to accept a one-bedroom condo without a den or second bedroom. She was adamant that she wanted the extra bedroom or den to display her collection. There was nothing on the market in a decent building and location that would match the criteria and when we analyzed the data it was evident that the price of what she wanted was not within reach for her with her current budget. She would have to compromise on something and only she could make the decision on what that something would be.

Would she compromise location for the space she had her heart set on? She could move west and get more bang for her buck, if the extra space is truly the top priority. Or was location more important than extra space? Perhaps it was the goal of home ownership, to plant the roots, to secure her financial future, to have something of her own, a starting point for future wealth and abundance that would be sacrificed. Narissa decided that location was more important than the den and said that she would sacrifice the extra room in order to achieve her goal, which meant we could look at the fabulous one bedroom condos that were on the market within her budget. She had successfully adjusted the plan, made a big decision, and we were on the road to making her dreams come true.

During the home buying process Narissa became discouraged very easily. She admitted that she was stubborn and seeing the reality of what she could buy challenged her resolve. We viewed a beautiful newer condo that had an extra-long bedroom with two long walls where Narissa could put the built-ins or shelving units that she had dreamed of to display her collection. As I described the potential, she seemed to like the idea. It wasn't the separate room she had envisioned but it was an excellent solution that would allow her to buy her home and showcase her collection beautifully. The condo offered an extra-large balcony that overlooked a residential neighbourhood with many trees and Narissa seemed excited that she could entertain her friends in her new home. After a few minutes Narissa lost her conviction and fell despondent. The reality did not match up with her ideal and although she had made the rational decision to forego the desire for a separate room she suddenly reverted to the old ideal. She was not handling the reality well, and she was not open to creatively solving her problem. The obstacles she was facing crushed Narissa's resolve.

Know there will be obstacles to overcome

Had Narissa focused on her goal and recommitted to it daily she would have overcome those obstacles. By connecting with her goal and her WHY she would have become more open-minded and open to opportunities that came up for her. To be open to opportunity you have to know precisely what your goal is and you must be creative in problem solving. I knew that home ownership was achievable for Narissa but I knew we'd have to massage her mind first. We would have to make sure that her goal was aligned with her true wants and that she was committed to achieving her goal. That commitment would allow her to be open to opportunity when it appeared.

Refusing to accept the facts and being closed to options is counter-productive. The obstacle you face is an obstacle to you alone and is not an obstacle to others who are also searching for a home to buy. The reality is . . . wait for it . . . you created the obstacle. You allow the obstacle that you create within your paradigm to stop you. You see, Narissa's friend believed that the long bedroom wall provided an excellent solution to the problem but Narissa's paradigm would not allow her to see it the same way her friend did. She was rigidly holding on to the plan she had created before she had become educated in the current market. Now that she was educated she needed to tweak the plan.

Align your vision with the facts

Narissa's budget was below the average price of a condo in Toronto. She would need to align her vision with the facts that were indisputable. Her mind was telling her that she should be able to get everything. She had worked hard, she had sacrificed to save enough money for a down payment, she had a secure job and earned enough money to finance a home purchase. She deserved it all. I believe that Narissa and anyone else who works toward a worthy goal deserves to achieve the goal. But wanting it all should mean wanting to achieve the goal. In her case the goal was to buy a condo where she could display books.

The real goal is always to feel good

If Narissa had been able to let go of the idea that the condo would have to look exactly the way she wanted it to look before she would feel good she would have been more likely to understand that she had the ability to feel good even though the den wasn't there. If she could have used the power of her mind then she would have experienced the freedom she thought the den would bring her. To say you create the obstacle is another way of saying you stop yourself from feeling good by not using the power of your mind to feel good.

Narissa had never owned real estate so it was difficult for her to imagine the feelings of owning her own place, the pride, the sense of accomplishment, the satisfaction when she opened up the door to her home, and the sense of safety. She did not attach those emotions to the dream. She would have to recognize what the real dream was before she could get it. If Narissa had spent the time working on her WHY list she may have been able to tap into the emotions. Instead, she allowed her emotions to become attached to the book display or the den and not the dream of home ownership. She determined that a den would make her feel good instead of knowing that the power of her mind could make her feel good. She blocked herself from the good feelings that were right there inside her.

It's hard to determine when your mind is giving you sound advice and when it's nonsense especially because the information the egoic mind holds is meant for survival and is all fear based: fear of loss, fear of judgment, fear of failure. There are some things that your egoic mind will tell you that are valuable. Like, you cannot fly so don't jump off the cliff without some sort of aid or equipment. Your egoic mind will yell, "Don't go too close to the edge of the 200-foot drop because you will die!" which is a good thing to hear. Your mind is designed to keep you safe, to help you survive. In that scenario, it is giving you valuable advice, and you should listen to it.

Flexibility is key, rigidly holding on to an ideal when the data suggest it's not wise is not serving you. It's a form of sabotage and even though you may tell yourself that you deserve better, the question is whether or not you are punishing yourself by holding yourself back.

Change the paradigm – change the behaviour

Narissa found the home buying experience was a much bigger challenge than she had expected. She had no experience with home buying and she thought it would be easy. The opportunity that presented itself was quite different from what she was expecting, and she was very frustrated. The frustration came from the paradigm that she needed the place to be exactly the way she had envisioned it before she knew anything about the current market conditions. She was closed and would not see the opportunities that presented themselves for her because she was too rigid and unbending. She was unwilling to make the compromises that were necessary to achieve the dream. She is going to have to change the paradigm before she can change the behaviour. She may believe it will be easy and that she'll get it all but the behaviour of refusing to see the opportunity that presents itself will not allow her to achieve her goal because the underlying cause, the paradigm has not changed. So was her real goal to upgrade her life, plant roots, build financial wealth and security? Or was it something else? Something did not align with the goal or the goal did not align with her paradigm.

As a casual observer, you can see that finding a beautiful condo that is within your very tight budget in a great location that offers a viable alternative to an item on your wish list is an amazing opportunity, and you would say you'd buy it. But when it's you, if your paradigm gets in the way you'll stop yourself.

Revisit and revise your wish list – be flexible

When you are searching for a home you have to constantly revisit and revise your wish list because you will have superfluous items on it that are not crucial to the dream. I could have turned down the pace car ride with Mario Andretti because it didn't look like my dream where I was actually driving an Indy car. My dream was to be on a race track with Mario for two laps, my dream was not to drive an Indy car. You see how specifically my dream manifested, as I was in a car with Mario for exactly two laps. It still blows me away that this even happened. Can you imagine if I had turned down the opportunity because it didn't look exactly like my vision? Do you think I might have regretted it? Perhaps I would have gone all these years without realizing that my dream had actually come true and that I had missed the opportunity.

You must be flexible to achieve your goals. I've noticed that when women buy real estate they do more planning than most men do and women tend to be less flexible about tweaking the plan. The plan has to be fluid to allow for the opportunities and to switch up when something fails or doesn't go as planned. By recommitting to your goal daily you will be able to make decisions easily when opportunities present themselves to you and you will know when it is time to stick to the plan and when it's time to bend a bit. Building the right support group will help you when you need to make these decisions.

When I asked if she would compromise, Narissa said yes and her compromise was to put the condo search on pause for a while and increase her savings, so that maybe she could get the type of condo in her dreams. Although she said the words that she would compromise, the reality was that she wasn't ready to make the right compromise in order to achieve her dream. She was stubbornly holding on to her ideal and was passing up the very real and very good opportunity before her. Narissa dealt with obstacles by digging in and not budging. To overcome obstacles when buying real estate it takes creativity and flexibility. You must have the ability to be flexible in the face of adversity. Her stubbornness may have served her well in the past but now it was setting her back. Stubbornly clinging to the ideal in her head made her unable to think on the spot or to make a decision that would serve her dream. Making decisions comes much more easily when you are very secure in yourself and when you know yourself extremely well. When you know yourself and you know your dream you can see the opportunities that are available to you.

Keep replacing until you find a workable plan

If your first plan doesn't work replace it with a new plan and if the new plan doesn't work replace it and keep replacing it until you find a plan that does work. When you come up against a brick wall tweak the plan but don't abandon the plan. Each time you work with a plan look at the opportunities that have presented themselves and decide if the plan is working or not. It may be true that the plan is working just fine but that you are blind to the opportunities.

Sometimes when you take a breather, you let the dust settle and everything becomes clear. I could see that Narissa had been really struggling with the search. She was disappointed in herself and was shocked at the difficulty. The disappointment she felt was misguided and she would need time to be able to clearly identify that her dream had come true but she hadn't seized it. The goal of home ownership still existed for Narissa but her top priority was to get it all and wait until she could afford everything she wanted before she would buy. In the meantime, the market outgrew her budget and she was unable to afford to buy a place that aligned with her ideal. She could either use the disappointment as fuel for a renewed commitment on a clear goal or she could allow it to create fear that could stop her from ever trying again. She would have to choose.

Start by truly caring how you feel

Narissa was determined and strong and if she focused her intentions she would succeed. She was apologetic to me but unnecessarily so because this was about her journey, her life and not mine. We can't worry about what other people are going to say or how other people will feel. Even though we have a very deep need for connection and a need for a sense of belonging we can't just throw out our ambitions because it won't align with what other people believe about us.

It can be very difficult to live authentically ourselves when our beliefs become very different from our family and friend's beliefs, our inner circle of the people closest to us. Sometimes it seems like we have to choose our relationship with our relatives over our own desires for ourselves. Once you begin to live your authentic self, the people around you begin to treat you differently because of how you treat yourself.

It causes pain when you push your own needs, desires, dreams down in order to fit in to everyone else's idea of who you are or who you should be. How long will you wait before you make the decision to address the real person within, to heal the person within who carries the burden of your parent's conditioning, their consciousness? If you are resistant to this you may be harbouring some resentment against someone, possibly your parents. You may be clinging to it because it's familiar and the thought of change is too scary. But you are living with the pain that comes with the resentment, anger, disappointment, and some of that may be directed at yourself. Perhaps you need to forgive yourself. We can easily get stuck in the blame game, blaming our parents for everything we are, how we act, our lost dreams, but they acted in the way they had been taught to act, they are the products of their own conditioning by society, culture, family, experiences. You don't have to take that on, you can be free of it, you can break the cycle. Start by truly caring about how you feel.

Nobody understands an entrepreneur except another entrepreneur

When you open a business or become a realtor you can't expect your family to be on the same page as you. They aren't speaking the same language as you, they don't have the same beliefs as you, and worse yet, they force the old beliefs on to you. They may say things like "You can't do that, don't you want to get married one day?" In a *Sex and the City* episode where one of the female lead characters wants to buy her own home she's told that she shouldn't buy a place because men would be threatened by her. The pressure is to conform, to forego the security of home ownership so that you can lower your energy to the level of the common person, to let go of your dream of becoming an artist/chef/pilot or whatever. "You can't do that, because none of us have. How dare you make us look bad? Your success reflects poorly on us. You should be just like one of us. Who do you think you are to dream so big, Miss Fancy Pants."

That's why you need a support group of like-minded individuals who can support you in your endeavours. Sydney had her realtor to rely on for support. Another woman I interviewed mentioned that she felt she could trust her realtor and attached herself to her energy and did accomplish the goal. The trust wasn't that deep and once she realized that the house she was to buy was sitting there waiting for her she went online and started looking in different neighbourhoods and different types of housing. This may also have been a symptom of perfectionism, fear of commitment, lack of confidence or fear of being judged and the fear of missing out or some other paradigm of hers.

I have found in my years of real estate sales that women tend to be extremely cautious, sometimes to the point of self-sabotage. Lack of confidence is one of the most common beliefs lend themselves to that factor. Men on the other hand seem to be much more confident. More confident that they will get the raise, the big job, more confident in decision making. So they don't buy real estate, and if they do, they make a decision quickly and have the attitude that they can handle whatever may come. That is very rare to find in a woman buying her first piece of real estate on her own. She checks with her support group and does even more due diligence in fear of making a mistake.

The plan and the real goal

How important is having a plan and when do you know to hold fast to each detail vs tweaking the plan or changing it radically or abandoning it all together? Start by understanding the purpose, the reason why this is a worthy goal. Be very clear on what the real goal is. My goal was to be on a track with Mario Andretti, it was not to drive an Indy car. Do this while you are in a state of peace, when you are calm. You need clarity in order to deal with the stress of buying real estate. You can meditate, listen to music, light candles and sit on the couch with your dog, or you can walk in the woods, sit by the ocean or get into the zone during your run.

"Take steps toward self-discovery."

You know what it takes to get to the state of calmness, which is when creativity happens. Even the tiniest drop of belief mixed with desire can send the message out clearly and in a way that will bring everything you need right to you. Take steps toward self-discovery.

Write out your personal mission statement, the purpose of the goal, what direction you are headed and what your motivation is.

What problems will owning your own home resolve and what problems will it cause if you don't own? Think on this and make a list. When you are tempted to give up on your dream or to be too demanding, review the list and refresh your commitment.

Tap into the passion, the emotion that you tie to the goal. Is it pride and a sense of accomplishment? How will you feel when you get home and put the key in the door, unlock it and step inside? What do you see? Who do you see? What does it smell like, is the sun shining, do you have the things you love around you? Will you be proud that you broke the cycle of your behaviour caused by your paradigms? What other emotions will you feel?

Hiring the right realtor allows you to focus on knowing what to do vs. how to do it. Your realtor is a master and knows how to do it.

Use emotional freedom techniques or clearing exercises when you feel the behaviour spinning you out of control. The frustration comes from believing you can change the behaviour before you change the paradigm. It can't be done that way, you have to start at the source of the problem and that is always your belief.

You can access your power at will

Develop courage by using your inner strength to overcome obstacles and to challenge limitations. You can access your power at will and become dependent on yourself and nobody else. You don't have to take crap from anyone. You do not need approval from anyone but yourself.

You should not allow a sense of obligation to hold you back. Analyze the situation to determine why you feel obligated and see if it serves you well. We have some obligations that we can't avoid, like taking care of our animals or children. There are other things that we allow ourselves to feel obligated to that are not important. We should truly understand our own needs and dreams and then determine whether or not we should break free.

Train your mind to work for you not against you, become unstoppable and make real choices. Get in the flow before you go out to view places or before you take each step of the way by using subliminal audio, meditation, reviewing your WHY list. Set the intention based on your true goal, the real purpose of owning your home.

When a guy does want to buy a place he doesn't let this kind of stuff stop him. His needs are basic. His goal is a place to crash and a place to build equity for now. Women buy forever (they think about a future baby, future partner), guys buy for right now. It seems that guys are better at living who they are right now and don't feel incomplete. They know that they are whole just as they are and they live in their power now. The women who are waiting for a partner or a baby are cheating themselves out of living right now.

In 24 years of selling real estate I've discovered that women tend to get caught up in the aesthetics and often miss opportunities because of it. Is this because women are judged on how they look and they fear they will be judged on how nice their home looks? Is it a fear of being judged that it is not enough, not good enough, therefore they are not good enough? Women often say it is because they have worked hard and so they deserve the best. I agree, everyone deserves to have everything they want but this belief can be dangerous if it becomes a form of self-sabotage and is not kept in check.

Are women just too picky, too brand aware? If someone is focusing on the brand name of a toilet for example they may not be truly in tune with the goal. I have seen this happen and my advice is to get a place and then buy any toilet you want. Don't let the brand name of something that can be easily replaced stop you from your goal of home ownership.

CHAPTER 14

Understand the Driving Force behind Your WHY

You may be one of those people who feel that they would like to own a home if it virtually falls in their lap. You think you really want it but in truth you're not willing to work hard for it, or to make sacrifices for it nor to plan for it. You may even plan for it, save money for it, but if you don't understand the driving force behind the WHY of it, you may sabotage your own goal.

Emily was a young woman in her late twenties who called me when she felt she was ready to buy a condo. She had come from Eastern Canada to work and live in Toronto. If you know Canada or if you know someone from the Maritime Provinces, you'll understand that these are two very different cultures, and growing up in one province gives you certain experiences and understanding of how the world works, while growing up in another province gives you a whole different perspective.

My husband and business partner Gary grew up in Charlottetown, Prince Edward Island. He came to Toronto during his early 20s and he shares his insight with me so that I've come to understand the differences. Having grown up in Toronto my whole life his insight has allowed me to see life with a broader view and has given me a deeper understanding of conditioning. I recognize how conditioned I am and how conditioned he is. This is good!

Back to Emily. She had lived in a rental with a roommate for several years, had achieved success at work, and had saved up a substantial amount of money for a home purchase. The amount she had saved was in excess of $180,000. That would allow her to purchase a property in the high $500,000s. Her desire to purchase was now being driven by three things:

1. Her roommate was moving out and she'd have to make some changes in her housing situation so it seemed like a good time to buy

2. She had enough money saved up now that she could qualify for a mortgage that would allow her to make a very decent purchase

3. A condo came up that appeared to be perfect for her

After our initial hour-long buyer consultation it seemed to me that Emily was on point, had planned and saved, had done research and envisioned herself living in a swank condo that she owned. She had spent years saving money for this day. We made plans to view the seemingly perfect condo.

Once we arrived at the condo building and viewed the suite we realized that it actually surpassed our expectations. This was a newer building that had recently registered as a condominium after being built. Until the building is registered as a condominium the lender will not be able to lend on the suites as ownership cannot be transferred out of the builder's name and into the mortgagee's name. As a result, there weren't any comparable sales within the building to help us determine the value. In order to set a value on the suite we took into consideration the location of the building, the condition of the building, the location of the suite within the building, and many features of the suite including square footage, parking, and more.

The suite was a popular item and there were many potential buyers with their agents viewing the suite at that time. We went to my office so we could talk freely after viewing the suite. We spoke for over an hour. Emily told me the many things she loved about the suite, how impressed she was and how she knew that it was perfect for her yet I could sense some hesitation.

We dug deeper to shed light on the doubts that were suddenly creeping up on her. Was it the wrong time to buy, would she lose money, should she buy or should she continue to rent, what if the building crashed, the market crashed, the economy crashed. She felt scared because all the money she saved would go toward the purchase of the condo and leave her with only $40,000 as a safety net. I recognized these fears and knew that she had a choice to allow them to sabotage her success or she could make the choice to move forward with the goal she had worked on for years. She was letting her old beliefs and her egoic mind keep her in the cell she had created in her mind. When the jail cell that holds you back is created from self-doubt the bars are tougher than titanium.

Of course you should think about all of those things, but you do that before you start looking at places. You shouldn't let those fears sabotage your success once you've found the perfect place. There isn't enough time to work through them before you lose the place to another buyer.

Go back to your list of reasons for buying

In the heightened state of fear it's virtually impossible to imagine yourself being in a calm state, which makes it impossible to be rational. This is when your list of reasons why you want to buy real estate becomes your tool for success. By reviewing the list you start to calm yourself and you recommit to your plan to buy real estate. Your renewed passion will allow you to overcome the obstacles that your mind is fabricating.

I started pushing buttons, making Emily understand that she was spinning out in fear and to breathe deeply, and to go deep into her own psyche, to see why she was doing this to herself. At the end of it, she sent me an email (they always write rather than talk) that she was questioning a real estate purchase in Toronto. Perhaps she shouldn't invest here after all, she wrote in her email. She wrote rather than called because she knew I'd call her out on her own bullshit. I wasn't able to help her overcome the last hurdle, the self-imposed obstacle, the story she made up in her mind. She had worked toward this goal for years, and she quit when she was one step away from winning.

Her dream may not have been home ownership at all. Perhaps she never envisioned herself in a beautiful well-located condo that she owned. She had made it to the finish line but did not allow herself to cross it because she could not see herself on the other side of it. She could not see herself on the winner's podium. When she created the dream of home ownership she had not envisioned herself succeeding. Perhaps she didn't believe she should could or that she deserved to be a homeowner due to some of her paradigms. Perhaps she was unable to picture herself happy and complete. She held on to the vision of having the money instead of the vision of owning her home.

Perhaps her dream was to save the money and to prove to herself that she could qualify for the financing to buy her own place. Perhaps she had become more attached to the idea of proving that she could do it than actually doing it. Maybe she had become addicted to seeing the money in her bank account grow and fell in love with idea of having almost $200,000 in the bank, saved up for a rainy day. Hell, who wouldn't love to have that money in their account? The problem was that she was fixated on having the money within reach and in what she believed was a safe place. She didn't see that the condo would become her safety net, that even if she lived there for years without an increase in price she would still be paying off her mortgage loan and would come out ahead at the end of it.

Think long term

Real estate is a long-term investment. Sure, you can flip properties and you can even make a lot of money doing it, but that is gambling. Go ahead and do it if you have the stomach (and bank account) for it. For the rest of us, buying a home should be looked at as a long-term investment, a place to live, a vehicle to build wealth. The real estate market is subject to change, it morphs from a strong seller's market to a buyer's market or a balanced market and with those changes come changes in value. In the U.S. there was a horrible housing situation that destroyed the financial health of many people. It's real. It can happen. I am not belittling Emily's fears. I am saying that she should have asked those questions and satisfied herself one way or the other before she felt cornered. She had backed herself into a corner where everything she had wanted suddenly was hers to take and she reacted like a terrified trapped animal.

Maybe she thought she'd never find her dream home so she had time to ease into the process of home buying and yet here it was. Her dream home was within reach, all she had to do was get it. It hadn't been a problem until the fear showed up, and she stopped herself short.

Why? Her thoughts that she should reconsider her decision of investing in Toronto real estate were something she could console herself with, something she could justify with family out east and friends here in TO, and with me, her realtor. That statement, "I am not sure I should invest in Toronto real estate" is something that would buy her time. I don't think it's my job to convince her to buy real estate in Toronto. I see my job as helping people who have made the decision to buy (or sell) real estate in Toronto to make informed choices on the road to successfully achieving their goal.

Her fear of a market crash was not supported by any facts. The media reported that housing was becoming too expensive for average people, and that prices just kept going up. The fact that Toronto was home to 130,000 or more new immigrants each year and that these people needed housing played a role in housing and this figure would grow every year. At that time, the story in the media was that not enough product was available and there were more buyers than homes in certain price points, Emily's price point specifically. I don't want anyone to go to the media for information on the market. Go to the source, go to the real estate board statistics. Emily made this stuff up as it wasn't even being reported by the papers that loved to use fear tactics on the subject of the Toronto real estate market.

For Emily, it seems her goal was just proving that she could buy but her WHY did not include home ownership. It only included the challenge of qualifying for a mortgage, of saving, of proving she could do that. None of her fears were supported by factual evidence as being a real threat. The one thing that stopped her from buying that perfect condo was her mind.

Money mindset

What are your thoughts on money? Have you ever delved into your paradigms around wealth? Your ideas most likely come from past experiences, things you heard your parents say, or the preacher. Let's examine them now because this is important.

You may have very positive healthy beliefs about wealth, and if you do that's amazing! Most people I know who are not incredibly wealthy do not have the most positive feelings around money. They never talk about it with friends, if family talks about money it's usually about not having enough and the conversation can get very heated. It's taboo to talk about money in many circles.

Many people teach you that money is evil. I believe that if you are evil when you're broke you will be just as evil with money. I believe that you can do much good with money should you choose to. I believe that utilizing negative ways to generate money, stepping on people, abusing power and stealing money from others is evil. Many people with great amounts of money do wonderful things with it and often in anonymity. Imagine the good you could do if you had unlimited resources and no limitations. What would you do, build an amazing orphanage where children are loved, very well taken care of and where they flourish? Would you fund an animal sanctuary? Would you build schools and wells for clean water? Would you feed kids and families in your own city, providing nourishing breakfast to kids who would otherwise go to school hungry, unable to focus and learn? Would you empower people who felt stuck in their lives? Would you help family and friends? Whomever you are right now is who you will be with money. You won't suddenly become evil.

"The universe is abundant. You create your reality."

Money is not as important as love, or happiness, or health. You may believe that you can't be spiritual and wealthy at the same time, that you can't be healthy and wealthy. Of course you can, you can be all three: healthy, happy, and wealthy. Rich people believe this, it is the mindset of rich people. You don't have to choose just one. The universe is abundant. You create your reality. You can have an abundance of love, of energy, of money and whatever you can dream. You can have it all. Do not limit yourself. Expand your vision, your list of wants, expand spiritually, choose beliefs that support your growth.

When you were little did you ask your mom for something, a new toy, new shoes and she told you to go to your father because he had all the money? It was common during the era that I grew up in that the man controlled the money. In this case, you may have learned that men had money and women relied on men to provide for them. Women don't have money. They depend on men. That feeds male paradigm, like the scene in *Sex and the City* Season 2 Episode 5: Miranda buys an apartment and Charlotte says, "If he still rents and you own, the power structure is off. It's emasculating. Men don't want a woman who is too self-sufficient."

So, you are only attractive if you are a little helpless/needy so you can feed his ego by allowing him to save you. He feels he is only attractive to you if you need his money, need him to save you. Being self-sufficient is a male trait (oh, but is it? How many of my friends handle the finances, make the whole thing work, carry it on their shoulders?). Carrie says, "They feel threatened because you don't need a man." You only need a man for money. Has real estate replaced pheromones? If you smell like real estate it means you are not a good mate? Imagine dating a guy and asking him how much money he has/earns because that was the only criteria you were interested in. He'd be insulted and would call you a gold digger, yet he places that belief on himself. Imagine the pressure of providing for everyone, like in the 1950s. It must have been hell. But yet, they cling to the paradigm, and we allow them to because that is our paradigm too. Women are expected to dig for gold and then are criticized for doing it. Men like to feel needed and then resent being needed for money. Take care of yourself and you are criticized, judged as the uncool friend like Miranda, and scary to men. What scares them, that you'll leave and they will be hurt? So they hold you down. And you let them.

You've heard the stereotype that women just spend money and can't manage it effectively. Do you spend the money as soon as you get it? If you get a bonus or some kind of windfall, do you blow the money right away? Then your paradigm is that you shouldn't accumulate wealth, that money is bad so you blow it. You deserve instant gratification, and you don't have a long-term goal for what the money is going to be used for, for example a down payment on a home and your financial freedom.

Focus on your most worthy goals

Save your money for a rainy day is commonly heard, and if you give too much energy to that you'll create the rainy day. The goal is the rainy day and you will achieve your goal. Do you see how this works? The mentality of scarcity keeps you there, in a position of lack. You feel that you had better save because you will need the money for some tragedy that will happen, because you believe that tragedies always happen to you. If you have this negative mindset you will find that tragedies always happen to you.

You may think, if I have a lot of money people won't like me, they'll want something from me, I'll pay too many taxes, what if I lose it all? That is your egoic mind, your deep-rooted fears coming up to strangle any hope of creating wealth and breaking you out of your status quo.

It's important to identify whether or not you respect home ownership, respect independence. Do you respect wealth? Do you respect choices? Reject whatever does not align with your most worthy goals.

Holy Crepe!

In 1996, I came home from a trip to Greece and decided I wanted to open up a little neighbourhood café and serve Belgian waffles and crepes with Nutella and bananas on them. I had seen this little hole in the wall on Mykonos, literally a small window where after the clubs you'd find a line-up as they waited for the most delicious and massive crepes with Nutella and other great toppings wrapped up in waxed paper and handed to them through the window. Off they went to enjoy their treats. At that time, Starbucks had not permeated our city so it was conceivable to open a little niche spot in a pedestrian-friendly neighbourhood. I had been looking for a new career and had not been accepted into law school as a mature student. The more I thought about what I wanted to do I knew I wanted to work with people and I thought about a cute little spot where locals could come and hang out, maybe read a book or magazine as this was before the internet was widely popular. See that? I created Starbucks in Chapters before it happened.

I called my agent and asked him to help me lease a spot along Bloor St. West in the Kingsway that I had my eye on. He reluctantly agreed and then asked why I wanted to work so hard. I replied with my favourite expression, "I want to work smart not hard!" He told me to go into real estate. I had been told before that I'd make a good realtor but I didn't know exactly what that meant. He kept talking, I said I didn't want to drive people around in my car, have their kids kick their dirty boots on the back of my seats and pick their noses and wipe it on my seats. He said, "So what, you show them 10 houses and you make $6,000. Do you know how many cappuccinos you have to sell to make that kind of money?" I knew how many. I asked how to get licensed as a realtor and the story goes on.

I did the licensing while I was working as a cashier at a popular breakfast spot near the airport on weekends and working at The Skydome as a hostess in a Sky Box to make ends meet. Both jobs were easy, allowed me to study for my exams, and paid the bills.

Help people your way

Once I had passed all of the course phases and exams I had been on my way 30 minutes west toward Mississauga to sign with a broker. I noticed that I had forgotten the required documents just when the phone rang. It was the broker in The Kingsway asking me to join his office. I was surprised because my impression had been that I was not good enough to be a Kingsway realtor. He said I was, so I joined his office. Once you signed with a brokerage you had to wait two weeks to receive your documents to be officially able to work as a realtor. I took the opportunity to go to my mom's condo in Florida knowing that I'd be working a lot afterward. I had a lot of time to think and I was terrified I would fail. I had no idea how I would find clients or if I would succeed in my new career.

While I was in Florida, I went out to the balcony one night. The Atlantic Ocean was as calm as a lake and there was a beautiful light coming from a full moon and it appeared to be coming right toward me. It was reflecting onto me as if I was performing a soliloquy on a dark stage. It caught my attention because it was so beautiful and unusual. As I looked at the unobstructed moon I saw clouds on either side that resembled herald angels with trumpets. A feeling of calm came over me and I received a message that I was on the right track, heaven was smiling upon me, this was exactly what I was supposed to be doing. I was calm and at peace, but in my thinking mind I was like, "as if!" I hardly thought that the heavens would rejoice because another realtor had been licensed but it made such an impact on me I remember it like it was yesterday.

During my second year as a licensed realtor, my friend called me to congratulate me on my success. I told her I wasn't happy and may not work in the industry for much longer. She asked me what I wanted to do. I told her I didn't know but I really wanted soul satisfying work; I wanted to help people. She said, "Oh my friend, you're missing the point. You are helping people." I said, "Yeah, yeah, I know, but I mean putting a key in the door and negotiating isn't what I want. I want to really help people."

She schooled me that day, my intuitive friend Pamyla. She said, "You are. You are helping people get to the next step in their lives, allowing them to fulfill a dream. Some will be able to start a family, others will move on to new relationships or start a business with the proceeds of the sale . . . so many things. And there's something in you that connects with them to help make it all happen."

I kind of fluffed her off, but the words stuck with me. The next day I showed a couple a house and the woman jumped up and down crying with joy and exclaimed, "I'm so happy we found this house because now we can have a baby!" I heard Pamyla's words in my head, saw exactly what she had talked about and suddenly I viewed my job through brand new eyes. Ever since then, I've loved my job and have done my very best to help people the best way I can. I've come to know the connection she mentioned and when the connection is not there the deal usually goes sideways. You can't bat a thousand.

Pursuing your goal isn't a hobby

Several years after I stopped doing TV and had focused on real estate and running a brokerage, I noticed that I was feeling a bit lost and felt I was floundering. I may have been a little depressed as well. I thought that perhaps I needed to develop some hobbies. I tried a few things, drawing and photography, but I wasn't passionate about the hobbies so I never gained any joy from either of those activities. My income had been declining steadily for a few years even though my activity had increased. I was working harder but I was making less money and I didn't quite understand what was going on.

In the summer of 2018, I reconnected with *Think and Grow Rich* by Napoleon Hill and recognized I did not have a goal. I was really surprised at myself because I had thrived with goal setting and I was a goal achiever. I thought back and realized that I hadn't really set a goal since 2004. After my health had dramatically improved I had set a goal in my mind to have a similar amount of money as my parents had had when I was a young girl. I even set the number in my mind. When the house next to the one I had grown up in became available I looked at it but decided it was not right for me because I wanted a house with a pool and soon one came up in the neighbourhood that was affordable.

Although it had many things I didn't like about it, I recognized that it was a fantastic opportunity, so I bought it.

Once I had achieved the goal I enjoyed it, gave thanks, and marvelled at having achieved my dream. I realize now that hosting 130 episodes of *Property Virgins* had allowed me to achieve the goal swiftly. I am very grateful for that. I could never understand why I had been selected for the host position out of the blue and even after having turned it down several times it pursued me. I understand now that it had allowed me to achieve the financial goal as well as my desire to help people.

So how did I go on for years without setting a new goal? I had gone into business with my husband and a couple of different partners over the years. My partners were not goal setters, and we weren't on the same wavelength on a few things. Eventually, both partners fell by the wayside. I recognized after the second break-up that I had been holding myself back. I had not allowed my power to shine through because I had allowed their paradigms to affect mine. I take full responsibility for this. I also recognize that I would have remained that way until the business had been lost. Thankfully, a shift happened and as soon as I realized that I was goalless I changed that immediately and began focusing on what I wanted. I had worked very hard in my life and it was time now to move into my power and create the life I wanted.

Make sure the goal is worthy

Living without a goal is not living, it is merely existing. You're either winning or losing. Staying with the status quo is losing. Just working toward a goal is winning, you are breaking through the status quo, you are not allowing the feeling of comfort to hold you back. Being comfortable keeps us from reaching out for what we truly want, from even taking the time to dream about what we really want. When you tell yourself you are comfortable you are really saying that it is convenient. Striving for a goal is not convenient so make sure the goal is worthy.

> "Celebrate achievement, pat yourself on
> the back, jump for joy, live in bliss."

I'm not saying that you can't celebrate and revel in the goals you have achieved, I want you to do that! I celebrated and enjoyed the lifestyle I had created for myself once I had achieved my goal and was very grateful for it. Celebrate the win! Celebrate achievement, pat yourself on the back, jump for joy, live in bliss. Once the confetti settles and gets swept away find a new goal. It will give you a reason to get up in the morning, will make you want to jump out of bed earlier and begin working on your new goal. It will give you vim and vigor, it's the best energy pill. You will be growing and perceiving life on a new level.

Without a goal you are not growing and in fact when I did not have a goal I was shrinking, my business was shrinking and my income was shrinking. The only thing that wasn't shrinking was my waistline. Been there? I know many have and I have to say that setting a goal motivates you in all aspects of your life and you find energy you didn't know you had. You discover opportunities you never saw before although they had always been there. Your personal life becomes happier. You become a more joyful person. You become the person you want to be and you will see that people who resonate with joy and happiness gravitate to you. In turn those people will support your dreams and you theirs. I hope that on my deathbed I still have a multitude of goals that I am working on because I know I will die happy. That sounds counter intuitive, but I know that if I am striving toward a goal I am a better version of me.

When I began working on determining my dream it took me months to be able to explore exactly what I wanted. I had fallen out of the practise of dreaming and goal setting and it took some time. I was in the paradigm that I was quite comfortable and had enough money for a nice retirement. It took some time to shake me out of that paradigm and a few others that were essentially holding me back from my own happiness.

Setting a goal is not an option for me, it is a must. When I am not working toward a goal I am stagnant and have low energy. I have set goals for myself that inspire me to jump out of bed and start working on them, goals that are always top of mind.

Through this work I created the desire to write this book so that I might inspire someone to work toward a dream. I had monthly sessions with a coach at the brokerage and she helped me stick to my goals. I shared *Think and Grow Rich* with some agents in my office, my stepsons, and my husband. I was back on track, and it felt great. By announcing my goals to like-minded people I enlisted help, and I was accountable. The coach introduced me to another professional coach because of my affinity to *Think and Grow Rich* and soon we were working together. My commitment deepened and as I write this I am still in the beginning stages of the work. I am so grateful for Napoleon Hill that if I ever get another bunny its name will be Napoleon.

How about group goal setting?

We recently set a group goal at the office and I can already see a shift in the excitement and commitment from the participating realtors. On the Wednesday that we set the group goal we decided that one of the rewards would be to find an office space that suited us better. We had previously had beautiful bright gallery-like space with high ceilings but were forced to move to make way for a new condo building. A space that was also very beautiful and located at the bottom of a new condo building became available and we negotiated for nearly two months but at the last minute, right before we signed the deal the landlord decided to lease it to his own real estate company. We were devastated because the space was now gone forever as you could not have competing businesses in the same location. We were unable to find suitable space that was affordable within our neighbourhood so we settled on an older darker space that allowed us to move with short notice as we were not tied down by a long term lease.

Within eight days of the group goal setting session I received an email letting me know that the space I had wanted four years before had now become available and was being offered to me first as a courtesy. It had taken only eight days to get us our dream space. It was putting the cart before the horse in the sense that the new office was supposed to be the reward for achieving the goal but when the opportunity comes you must act immediately. We viewed the space within 24 hours and signed the letter of intent within days. Carpe diem, baby!

I understand why it did not happen for us four years prior. It was because I was not in the right head space to take on the location. The business would have failed or perhaps it would have succeeded but I would still be holding back with a partner that just didn't vibe well and I would not have set new goals. I would have stagnated for way too long and it would not have served me well.

Growth only comes when you are uncomfortable

When we decided to lead the agents in my office to success by setting a group goal, I knew that it would not resonate with some of them and some would feel threatened because their egoic minds would tell them it was dangerous, they wouldn't need that, it was not right for them. I knew I would lose some of them because the timing just wasn't right for them to change their own paradigms and I was okay with that. Knowing that growth only comes when you are uncomfortable and knowing that many people never stretch themselves to allow growth I expected to lose some agents. Staying comfortable won't make you successful. Goal achievers are willing to do the things that their counterparts won't do. That's what makes them achievers and empowered. Sticking with what is familiar is the safe way to live. This does not empower you, in fact it holds you back. Beware of the story your mind tells you.

"Beware of the story your mind tells you."

I knew that the new paradigm of success consciousness in our company would empower the remaining agents to lead fuller richer lives and we would have a core group of goal driven people. A new goal of mine was born.

How to set a goal

Napoleon Hill's *Think and Grow Rich* helped me get back on track and reinvigorated my energy, got me going on track to write this book and to work toward many other goals. I gave copies to my family and recommended it to my agents and friends.

Hill describes step by step how to set and achieve goals. I truly hope you will pick up a copy that includes the original text. The revised version removes the word ether from the book, and reduces its effectiveness, but please get a copy and read it cover to cover over and over again. Now I just read a few of my favourite chapters, a few pages per day, and every day I get an idea, or I get inspired to do the things I need to do in order to achieve my dreams. It's my favourite tool and I cherish the copies I have.

"Get out of the habit of losing and
get into the habit of winning!"

I have a boutique real estate office with only a few agents and one year one of the women who worked with us planned a team building activity for us. It would raise money for a cause I believe in and we'd have a blast as a group of like-minded people. She decided we would climb the CN Tower. The tower had been the tallest free-standing structure in the world until 2007 at 553.3 metres, with 1,776 steps, 144 flights of stairs. As you stand at the base of the tower waiting for your start time, you wonder how you will achieve climbing 144 flights. One step at a time, one flight at a time. Then it's time, and off you go. Before you know it, you've completed one flight, then two, then 20, 50, 100. You can't quit now! You keep going until finally all 144 flights are behind you, and you're at the top. There's a team waiting to congratulate you and record your time on the back of your t-shirt. My time was very slow, but I made it and nobody can take that success away from me. It was a big win for me. Because of my lung issues, climbing stairs and steep inclines is challenging for me. The feeling of winning changes your biochemistry. You should spend time reflecting on a big win, either past or future and train your brain to create more wins. Get out of the habit of losing and get into the habit of winning!

You need to spend some time really thinking about what you want. It's not easy, especially when your mind gets in the way. Ask yourself what you would want if nothing was impossible and if you had every resource you needed in order to get it. This can take some time, and as you progress, you'll find that you tweak this or that, and you begin to write out a beautiful story of who you will be when you achieve the dream. When I started to dream in the fall of 2018, I wrote out in a notebook everything that came to mind when I said I wanted a new goal. It took me about two months to nail it. Goals invigorate me and when the dream I had written failed to inspire me I recognized that it was not the right goal. As I type this, I just misspelled goal as gaol, which in Britain means jail. So this came to mind: if you don't have a goal you are keeping yourself in gaol (jail). I know this to be true.

Focus on what gives you joy

Work on this awhile and find what you can become emotional and passionate about. It really does have to inspire you. Become inspired, sit and meditate, look on to nature or walk in nature without your earbuds on. Listen to the birds chirping, the sound the river makes, the waves of the ocean or lake. Focus your eyes on the flame of a candle, or a spot on the wall. Do whatever it takes to get into the zone. Focus on what gives you joy. It gives me joy to envision a mare with her foal kicking up its heels in the pure joy of living, in a green field, sun shining, weeping willow and babbling brook. That vision calmed me, centred me, and rejuvenated me in my darkest times when I was younger. Find one that works for you or sign on to one of the many wonderful and free meditation apps.

When I was doing this work I was on Instagram and saw an ad for Oprah and Deepak offering a 21-day free guided meditation. To this day, I've never seen it since, and luckily I seized the opportunity immediately and I am so grateful that I did as I found it very helpful. Napoleon Hill tells you to act on opportunity immediately otherwise you will doom your own success. He is referring to the fact that your ego will get in the way and that the inspiration came to you as the universe provides everything you need in order to achieve your goal.

This is who I am!

It seemed like Deepak knew what I was thinking and then spoke on it the following day. That's not coincidence, it's opportunity. It's the ether, the vibration attracting exactly what I needed to help me achieve my goal. If I had missed the opportunity, allowed my paradigms to come back into play and tell me I was fine as is, I didn't need more, to want more was greedy and so on, I would have missed the opportunity that was presented to me. Hey, maybe there were a number of other opportunities that I missed at that same time because I was just learning to believe. Who knows! I know this: I will be given opportunities again and will act on them. I know this because I am focused and work each day on achieving each of my goals, and my list of things I want to achieve continues to grow. I recognize that this is my new life, that I must work on myself, on feeding my mind the right thoughts, on dreaming and achieving every day as long as I live. This is who I am. I am living my authentic self and I hope you are too.

This one day I was relaxed and focused on meditating on the goal vision I had created and suddenly I felt a little twinge of something. I recognized it from the day before and the day before that. It caught my attention and I stopped to reflect upon it. What was it? I shed light on it and I realized that it was fear. I knew it would sabotage me if I didn't address it so I shone light on it until it came clear. This all happened pretty quickly, a matter of seconds. My desire to know and to achieve my dream was bigger than any irrational thought so I pushed through it. It came to me that I was afraid that when I achieved my dream, people would hate me, they would not like or love me anymore. I laughed out loud. I recognized it as being ridiculous and I also understood that I had already dealt with that. When I became successful in real estate some people around me couldn't cope with it at first. Remember the story about when I was on *Property Virgins* and how people close to me couldn't handle my success. So my ego was trying to tell me to shrink myself to a size that would feed other people's paradigms. I simply refused. I laughed, said, "Thanks for showing up but that is just hogwash" and released the fear. It never came up again. I knew I was achieving my dream.

It wasn't long after that that evidence began to show up. Evidence means there are signs that the pieces to the massive puzzle are being pulled into place like a magnet pulls iron filings toward it. I was the magnet and the universe had millions of iron filings that it was allowing to be drawn to me in order to fulfill my dream.

The first step – focus on what you really want

To recap, the first step I had to take was to focus in on what I really wanted. It wasn't easy and to do it right it took time. It may feel strange to allow yourself to dream without limitation and to think about what you want because it may be the first time in your life that you have given yourself permission to do so. You will deal with many paradigms and to help you deal with them you should keep a running list of all the things you want, and all the reasons that pop up on why you can't have it. The reasons why you can't have them are irrational, not true and are made up excuses. You will discard the sheet of paper, but before you do write out the opposite to each of the paradigms. If the paradigm is that you don't deserve it, write out, "I am worthy of this and more."

Review the list of things you want, meditate on it daily or even more often until you believe that you will have it. Once you've nailed it, write it out as a command. State what you will have or accomplish, set a date very specifically, i.e not in a little while but give it a date: by May 6, 20XX.

Set micro goals

Once you make a plan on how to achieve the goal you will have a number of steps that you will need to take to get there. For example, if you are in sales and your goal is to earn a certain amount of money you will state that you are prepared to make the calls you need to make each day, Monday to Friday and will not allow any distractions to take your focus away. You will do whatever it takes to achieve this micro goal. Know what you are prepared to do to achieve your goal, what you will give. If you are in business, you will have a business plan with marketing activities, income-producing activities and more. You will break it down to determine the number of calls, number of clients, number of sales you need in order to make your goal. These are your micro goals.

If your goal is to buy a home you will have to save enough money for a down payment, you will have to improve your credit score, you will have to earn a certain income in order to qualify for financing. So your statement will include for example, I will save $1,000 per paycheque, I will pay my bills on time and reduce my debt. I will increase my earnings by 10 per cent, and I will focus on my goal each day by spending 30 minutes envisioning my life once I have attained my goal. Whatever it will take, command yourself to do it and follow the order.

During the phase where you wrote things down that you wanted, you started to hone in on one or two things that were really important to you, like owning your own home. This became a burning desire for you. It never left, it only grew. It makes you smile when you dream about it, you think about it several times a day, you look at properties for sale online, you research certain buildings and neighbourhoods and you watch real estate shows. You really want this.

Eliminate all doubt

The next step in the goal-setting process is crucial to your success. You need to believe with every bone in your body that you will have it and these steps will help you develop this belief. To do this you have to eliminate all doubt. Any twinges or resistance that come up when you think about it are doubts, fears, paradigms that must be eliminated immediately. When they come up, you can choose to:

1. Bury them back down to come out to haunt you for the rest of your days or until you deal with them.
2. Believe them and let them stop you right there.
3. Release them as nonsense and replace them with the opposite positive belief. I am worthy, I am doing this, I am limitless.

You can't stop negative thoughts from showing up but how you deal with them is up to you. Choose to control your thoughts or let your thoughts control you. Hint: choose #3!

Read aloud your command a minimum of twice per day. Do it while dancing in your bathroom, do it while running, do it with joy. Do it before and after meditating. Some people find they gain more belief if they read it before they meditate, it sets the tone of their meditation. Others find it works to do it immediately after meditation because they are open and calm. I have recorded myself reading my command passionately and I listen to it during meditation as well as other times of the day. Find your groove with this and do it often. Repeat it, rewrite it, post it to the mirror in your bathroom, on the fridge, on your phone and computer screen saver. Obsess over this.

Attach emotion to your dream

Attaching emotion to your dream is a great way to fast track it. If you envision the dream without the vibration of emotion you may not be working toward the true dream that you have. Go back to your list of why you want it that we made in the earlier chapter. Review those words, the reasons why you wanted it. If you did the exercise correctly by following the instructions you will find the emotions in those words. Tap into them and revise your goal so they align and resonate with each other and with you.

Now you are ready to create a plan of action. Number one: be open to opportunity. It may not come in the manner you want it to, and it may even seem a bit challenging at first, but trust yourself, be open, and act on it immediately.

I was working on my book goal and part of my dream entailed a business I wanted to start that encouraged young girls to dream and step into their power. I had it scheduled to happen after I had finished my book and had it published but one evening while speaking to my friend Pamyla she once again opened my eyes to opportunity. She mentioned a woman we were acquainted with who was doing some fabulous work and suddenly an understanding occurred. I knew the woman we were talking about would be a perfect person to work with for the business I had scheduled for later. I thanked Pamyla and began researching the woman only to discover that she was more than perfect for the project. I told myself I'd reach out to her once the book was finished.

I went to Florida about five days after that evening with the intention to focus on the book and completing it. I took a break and went outside during my second week in Florida and was reading *Think and Grow Rich* in the sun. I came across the passage that said you must act immediately upon the inspiration that comes. He writes, "Be on the alert for these plans, and when they appear, put them into action immediately. When the plans appear, they will probably 'flash' into your mind through the sixth sense, in the form of an 'inspiration.'" He goes on to say, "Treat it with respect, and act upon it as soon as your receive it. Failure to do this will be fatal to your success."

I reflected on this passage. It dawned on me that I had not acted on the flash of understanding I'd had. By now, it was two weeks later and I jumped up, went inside, found that woman's contact info and wrote an email. It was not well thought out, it was typed quickly and without planning, but guess what! She was on her computer at that exact moment and responded within three minutes! We had a telephone conversation two minutes later and I explained with passion what I had been planning for the future, but I realized the time is now. Again, I didn't have a pitch put together or a proposal but she was very interested and we made an appointment to meet and discuss when I returned to Toronto.

My old paradigm held me back and had convinced me that I could only deal with one aspect of the dream at a time. That belief had almost crushed my dreams by causing me to wait until I was "ready" to approach her. Napoleon Hill said to treat the flash of inspiration with respect and to act upon it immediately. I understand that the universe works at lightning speed and I must respond in kind. I visualized an umbrella, and under the one umbrella were all of my business ventures including, but not exclusively the book and the girl's empowerment venture, as well as a pro-bono service I dreamed of offering to the world.

Take action immediately

You must take action immediately! If you don't, you will never achieve the goal. You can't win the lottery if you don't buy the ticket. Make the decision and stick with it. Don't allow the opinions of others to sway you. Be persistent, keep this goal top of mind. You will begin to see opportunities that you had overlooked prior to honing in on your goal. Be grateful for your blessings now and give thanks for the ones you are dreaming of as if you are already in possession of them.

"Be grateful for your blessings now and give thanks for the ones you are dreaming of as if you are already in possession of them."

Once you have your plan nailed down, and you are executing it as well as you can, you may find that things are not working out the way you had planned and everything is a struggle. First step, check your dream. Is it still the thing you dream about in the night and during the day? Then, ask yourself if you have done all of the things you know you need to do in order to achieve the goal. If you can honestly say that you've done the work, made the calls, saved the money, etc. it may be time to tweak the plan.

Be honest with yourself

Don't allow the old paradigms to sneak in and rob you of your goal, rob you of your power. If an obstacle has arisen, find a way around it. Do not allow outside circumstances to steal your dream. People who are committed to a dream will find a way to overcome any and all obstacles along the way. Beware that oftentimes the road is at its bumpiest and darkest right before a major breakthrough, so don't allow your egoic mind to trick you into giving up. When I say you should tweak the plan I mean you should hire someone new, get a more supportive group of people who understand your dreams and applaud you, change your marketing plan or your sales pitch. Do not change your dream. If your dream is home ownership and you discover that you cannot afford a one bedroom plus den condo with parking and stainless steel appliances in the neighbourhood you love, you must understand that there are practical ways for you to get your condo. You can forego purchasing the parking spot and opt to rent one instead, bringing the purchase price down significantly in some cases, allowing you to get the other things on your list. Or, you get the condo with white appliances and set a new goal to buy all new appliances to your liking by a certain date, then make the plan and get them. Or satisfy yourself with a lovely one-bedroom condo and work toward trading up in a few years.

Use your imagination and be open to opportunity. There are ways to work around the obstacles that you create. Yes, you create them. It may not seem that way, I know, but it is commonly known that we create our own lives including the good, the bad, and the ugly.

Don't give up, create the habit of finishing what you start. Be persistent, never give up. Tweaking ain't quitting.

CHAPTER 15

How to Buy a House

Single mother Patti had only a few months left on her mat leave and knew she needed to find and buy a place soon so she could start looking for local daycare services for her daughter. She wanted to buy a home so she could build equity for her family and owning property would provide financial security.

We talked about her wish list and what she envisioned as home. She was torn between quality of investment and quality of life. She craved a pedestrian-friendly location to suit her preferred lifestyle. She had lived in the suburbs in the past and was not loving the vibe. She wanted something more urban where she'd be close to everything Toronto has to offer. She knew if she moved further away from the city she'd be able to pay down her mortgage more quickly and that was creating a dilemma for her.

While we were working together I noticed that Patti had no idea what her budget should be. She hadn't calculated her expenses and her income and had only the amount the lender had agreed to. She hadn't considered maintenance fees and property taxes. She hadn't yet focused on affordability. I coached her about the expenses and encouraged her to work the numbers to find the sweet spot. When you are in this position you must take into account every fixed expense and the cost of the lifestyle you enjoy. Be careful not to leave yourself short each month and plan to have a surplus.

She said she was afraid to do her numbers because she was afraid to actually find out what she could truly afford. She didn't want to be disappointed. That is brutally honest of her and honesty is what is needed. I just couldn't move forward until she broke through the fear barrier and calculated her financial situation. She discovered that she could afford more than we had thought. This was based on fact and not rationalization. She could now purchase the condo she loved and realized that the maintenance fee was higher than other buildings we had looked at because they included all utilities and cable TV.

She joked that while she was waiting to hear what happened with the offer she wanted to back out. It was a joke but for some people it becomes very real and they do back out of the deal. The egoic mind gives it one last effort to stop you from breaking free of the old paradigms. Patti was successful in securing her future and the baby's future. The monthly cost was affordable for her, which put both of us at ease. It just took some research for it all to become clear.

Buying a place was the hardest thing she ever had to do. Coming from a single mom that says a lot. She feels proud that she can be a role model for her daughter who will grow up knowing that Mom bought property on her own. When she grows up she will be able to do the same thing.

"Ladies, figure out your numbers and just go out and do it! I've come into myself a little bit more now that I have my own place. It's no longer just a fantasy or a dream. It's real." —Patti

---

Some of our many false beliefs

Okay ladies, it's time to call out some of the false beliefs that limit us, that define our false reality, and hold us back from life in general and from buying real estate.

Feeling responsible for everyone else

We hold ourselves back in part because we believe (often correctly) that people will be jealous of us and we don't want them to have those negative feelings. Our concern is not what we want or what is right for us, instead it is how to protect them from our shining light, our power. We tell ourselves that if we buy our own home or investment properties they'll feel like we're showing them up, which will remind them of their failure, and we don't want to be the cause of their discomfort. Guess what, it's them, not you! If they feel uncomfortable in your light they are the ones who need to deal with their own paradigms. The women who think they should not buy a home because the future Mr. Right might not like it, feel responsible for how some person they've never met will feel. Remember what Marianne Williamson said, "There is nothing enlightened about shrinking so that other people do not feel insecure around you." Don't shrink yourself, ever. Instead, keep expanding, growing, and flourishing, always. Buy your own home, love your own home, watch your wealth grow with your own home, and stop worrying about everyone else.

Hard questions to ask yourself:
- What purpose do the people I am protecting serve?
- Do I want people in my life that are based on my remaining small so they feel comfortable?
- Am I addicted to the feeling of being controlled by their paradigms?

Thinking it's our job to fix everyone else

As fixers, we want to be there for everyone to fix issues at every opportunity. However, it often gives us the ability to avoid dealing with our own needs. Our need to be fixers comes from a belief of unworthiness. We try to develop value by allowing people to rely on us to fix their problems and thus enhancing their perceived value of us. By being there to fix everything for them we believe we are giving them a reason to love us. It is very difficult for a fixer to say no to someone in need but it is crucial that we train ourselves to look after ourselves first. Of course, you are going to help by supporting or encouraging, empathizing with people in our families, circle of friends and people at work, but we have to recognize that our needs should not be ignored, and that we should not expend all our energy and time on others.

Stop using this as an escape mechanism or a way to procrastinate from pursuing your goals and taking that courageous step towards your dream of home ownership. There is also an element of control at work here. We want to control things, and it seems easier to control someone else's dilemma than to deal with our own because we are at arm's length, and we can avoid the truth about ourselves. To break the habit of being The Fixer, start building boundaries and encourage others to learn how to cope with life issues. Put your own oxygen mask on first. Let it go, girl, work on yourself now.

Hard questions to ask yourself:
- By expecting them to be 100 per cent of what I want them to be, how am I making them feel?
- Am I empowering them or am I limiting them?
- Do I want to limit them or do I want to empower them to be who they truly are?
- What am I avoiding?
- What truth about myself am I trying to ignore?

Perfectionism

The need to be perfect is dangerous and limiting because we impose restrictions upon ourselves. Striving for perfection makes you imperfect, so drop it. Stop imposing restrictions on yourself and begin liberating your dreams without the fear of falling short of your own expectations and those of the people around you. We have the fear of looking like a fool by publicly making a mistake and are so afraid of making a mistake that we don't ever get started. You won't even allow yourself to try in fear of allowing others to see your flaws and that limits you drastically. You are afraid to expose your weaknesses without realizing that people can see through you already and know you have faults, perhaps the biggest one is your need for perfection.

> "Stop imposing restrictions on yourself
> and begin liberating your dreams
> without the fear of falling short."

Everyone has an opinion on real estate, and they won't hesitate to tell you that you did it wrong. They will criticize the location, size, finishes, price and more, which will expose your inferiority. You can't handle that because you feel superior to everyone around you or quite the opposite, you feel inferior so you strive for perfection as a way to avoid being judged. Perfectionism is detrimental, anti-productive, discourages growth and progress, and limits the definition of success to an unrealistic standard that will never be achieved because it is constantly changing so you believe it's better to not even try. Perfectionism holds you back from buying a home because you wonder if a better one will come around tomorrow, gives you a fear of commitment lest you be judged for choosing the wrong one.

Hard questions to ask yourself:
- Why am I afraid of making a mistake?
- What is the worst that can happen?
- Who will I become if I make a mistake?
- Who will I feel inferior to if I make a mistake?

Blaming yourself for your good fortune

There is no luck, you create your own reality. It may be that people say you were in the right place at the right time, however, the truth is that you were open to opportunity, recognized it and took it. The very same opportunity may have presented for them but they were closed to it or were too afraid to take it. Those people may react very badly to the perceived good fortune of finding and buying your dream home successfully. If you hold back to avoid their bad mood or nasty words you are buying into their paradigm instead of your desires. It's them, not you. You should embrace all of the abundance that the universe holds for you. Start by focusing on what you really want regardless of what they want for you. You'll be much happier in the long run and happiness is what it's all about. You deserve to be happy, fulfilled, and to achieve your goals.

Hard questions to ask yourself:
- Why do I shrink myself and allow this person's bad behaviour?
- What would happen if I discouraged the bad behaviour and made it known that it is no longer accepted?
- How does the behaviour of this person serve me?

Believing you don't deserve it, you're not worthy

You may feel unworthy because at some point in your life someone else got something you felt you deserved, or you never got enough attention from someone and that made you feel unworthy. You feel like you come from the wrong side of the tracks and would be called Miss Fancy Pants if you expected to own your home or many properties. You've been told you can't, and that you shouldn't do certain things and you've internalized the feeling that you don't deserve it. You hold yourself back because you don't want to shine too brightly so you adopt the status quo and shrink yourself to what you perceive is the acceptable level, always keeping an ear open for someone to remark negatively and when they do you shrink even more and it justifies your false belief. Of course you are worthy, of course you deserve home ownership. Don't let anyone tell you that you can't or shouldn't own your home. Why would one person deserve to own a home and another would not? There is no reason, so stop the negative self-talk and go get what you want.

Hard questions to ask yourself:
- Who taught you to believe that you are not worthy?
- Why did they do that, what was their paradigm?
- Does that paradigm serve you at this moment?

Procrastination

We procrastinate when we are afraid and when we become overwhelmed by the task list. Procrastinating only prolongs the stress and makes the situation worse when it comes time to act. We know this from experience, but the habit needs to change, the belief associated with it has to change before we will see better results. You may be telling yourself that you can't do it or some other negative false belief. Write out the false beliefs and then follow up by writing out the exact opposite right thinking. The complexity and required decision-making causes you to feel helpless so you put it aside for later. To work through this, break it down into tasks and tackle one at a time:

1. Get help from a professional
2. Get credit rating
3. Determine where your money has been going
4. Make a plan to save money
5. Talk to people who have done it successfully.

Warning: be careful not to become too involved with the idea of doing only small tasks, and avoiding the more challenging ones, the ones that will land your goal within reach. This can become a creative form of procrastination, i.e. looking at listings of homes for sale online but not enlisting the help of a realtor deludes you into thinking you are actively pursuing your dream but you are not.

Hard questions to ask yourself:
- What will I gain by procrastinating?
- What will it cost me if I procrastinate?
- What emotions am I feeling?
- What is really holding me back?
- What negative feelings and thoughts am I having?
- What action can I take today to get me moving toward my goal?

Believing you don't have to do it right now; there's no rush

When we say, "I don't have to do it right now," or "I can't be bothered" we are just being lazy and possibly delusional. We tell ourselves we're fine because we're comfortable no matter the circumstances. We live in denial that things aren't as great as they could be. When someone mentions that it may be a good idea to buy a home you say, "Yeah, but . . ." and continue with a list of excuses why you should delay. "Yeah, but . . ." will get you in the butt in the long run.

Your excuses are never the reasons why. The truth lies in the reasons, not in the excuses. Review the list of why you want to own a home and the things that will happen in your life if you don't own a home. Be careful not to rationalize your way into the trap of thinking things like, "I'll keep renting to save more money" even though you already have enough saved up. The value of the money is reduced over time by inflation. You may not be able to save at the same rate as prices are increasing, mortgage interest rates may go up and your money will not go as far as it used to.

Hard questions to ask yourself:
- Am I scared of the process or the result?
- What is really going on in my head?
- What am I truly afraid of?
- Am I hiding in my comfort zone and afraid to break free?

Being afraid of the outcome and having a fear of success

We are scared of success because it means we will have to deal with the change from being unsuccessful to being successful, how people will react to our success, and having to manage all of our abundance. The idea of this is way too frightening for us and with this belief we don't allow ourselves to grow. Our fear of rejection (they won't like me anymore) holds us back. Those people will either rise up to meet your new healthy attitude or not, but you cannot control it and you should not allow the fear of it to control you. Going from the comfort zone of being an underachiever to the frightening prospect of being an achiever will cause shock and awe in others and within yourself. Once you taste victory in achieving your goal, you'll always crave it. Owning your own home can be one of the most rewarding things you ever do for yourself and training yourself to set and achieve goals is vital to a happy life.

Hard questions to ask yourself:
- What will happen when I succeed?
- How will I feel about myself when I am successful?
- Who is holding me back?
- Should I give in to the false belief that I should not progress in life?
- If people reject me because I am successful should I become unsuccessful again just to make them happy?
- Am I simply assuming they will not be able to deal with my success, and should I give them the opportunity to accept me when I am successful?
- If those people truly do reject me are they really the best people to have in my life in that capacity?
- Can I maintain a relationship with them with new boundaries that I define?

Lacking motivation

If you know you should pursue this goal and yet you suffer from low motivation it may be because you have unclear goals, and you have a low self-image. It's time to review your goal to make sure you are aligned with it. Be sure to tap into the emotion of the dream, and if it doesn't resonate with you it may not be the right goal. Perhaps you're afraid because you have failed in the past and you're afraid to try again, you're afraid to fail all over again. Perhaps you are surrounded by negativity, and you lack confidence. Review the reasons why you want to buy property and what you really want. By reconnecting with the reasons why you want to buy real estate and feeling the emotion of it you will find the motivation that will take you to the next step, which may be finding the right support group and distancing yourself from the madding crowd.

Hard questions to ask yourself:
- What do I really think of myself?
- Do I have a positive self-image or can I improve on it?
- Do I believe that I am worthy of self-love?
- What do I really want for myself?
- Why don't I go get it?

Feeling a lack focus

We can lose our focus due to fatigue from the grind of our everyday lives and when our goal is a big one and it's taking time to achieve it. We can also lose focus when we are faced with many fun distractions like girls trips, destination weddings, wanting a new car. Find ways to keep on track and budget for trips and weddings as well as real estate. It entails being realistic with your budget, what you spend, and deferring gratification to achieve a worthy goal. You can also make mini goals that will lead to the realization of the big goal of home ownership. A mini goal can be opening up a special bank account for saving a certain amount of money towards the down payment of your new home.

Hard questions to ask yourself:
- Why do I allow small obstacles to throw me off track so easily?
- Have I nailed my goal or is it a work in progress?
- Am I committed to my goal?
- Am I concerned about what people will say if I opt out of fun activities in the name of my goal?
- If so, how is this serving me well?

Not knowing where to start

This feeling can lead to overwhelm, but here are a few suggestions that will get you moving. Making and reviewing a list of reasons why you want to own real estate is a good place to start. Talk to a professional realtor and a mortgage consultant to learn about the home buying process. A professional will give you a list of actions you can take right away that will get you working toward your goal. Make inquiries about borrowing money, analyze your spending by tracking what you spend each month with fixed and other expenses. Decide what you are willing to give up to achieve your dream. Be honest and realistic and then commit to it.

Hard questions to ask yourself:
- Do I believe I am worthy of this goal?
- Do I believe the goal is worthy of me?
- What small actions can I take this week that will get me moving toward my goal?
- Have I been faced with difficult challenges in my life and if so how did I deal with them? What were the results?
- What can I learn about myself from those experiences that I can apply to home buying?

It's too hard, it's not meant to be

Almost nothing worthwhile is easy. Believing that if it's meant to be it will just fall into your lap keeps you from being accountable for your actions. We expect home buying will be easy and as soon as it gets a bit challenging, we back away from our dream. Believing that if it's meant to be it will be easy hinders your ability to make changes in order to grow and reduces the chances that we will recognize opportunity when it appears. You have to buy the lottery ticket before you can ever win the jackpot and just claiming that it wasn't meant to be when you didn't win the lottery is nonsense. You have to take action, you have to seize opportunity, you have to create the circumstance.

Hard questions to ask yourself:
- If I am not accountable for my life who is?
- Am I rationalizing?
- Why do I expect everything to just fall into my lap?
- Why am I afraid to work toward this goal?
- What is really holding me back?

Thinking it's more important to be right than happy

You think that the right home will jump up and hit you in the head and when no perfect place becomes available within your criteria. You think it's because it's still out there and that's the one you deserve and "I'll show you that I can get it!"

I want you to get it all, but thinking that you can control everything so you can get perfection is not helpful, it's harmful. It's the dream that the perfect place will magically appear exactly how we envisioned it and being able to control this is we have to let go of and we feel that letting go of control makes us weak. When we can be open to new ideas we will be bothered less by the minutia or even the things we thought were hugely important to us, like stainless steel appliances. We become more accepting of things when we stop trying to control results. If you don't address these beliefs you will allow bad experiences or wrong thinking to take up the real estate in your mind so that there is no room to introduce right thinking, positive thoughts even when you know you are wrong. You hold on to this story even when you know it's wrong. When you are able to seize opportunity when it presents itself you will be right, right as rain.

Hard questions to ask yourself:
- How does this serve me?
- How does clinging to my story hinder me?
- Will I achieve my goal if I cling to my story?
- Why do I feel I have to be right? Is my happiness something I am willing to sacrifice just so I can be right?
- What does happiness look like to me?
- How will I feel once I achieve my goal?
- What if I'm wrong, what would be the worst that could happen?
- Could I handle it?
- What would be my options at that point?

Fear of the unknown

Most of us are afraid of the unknown and only some of us will embrace it in order to step out of our comfort zone and into the realm of success that was previously unknown to us. Nobody can predict the future, and life has a way of happening regardless of how in control we feel. You are afraid to take action because it may uncover a truth you don't want to know. Be true to yourself, that's where happiness lives. You may be afraid that action will take you outside of your comfort zone. Being comfortable isn't being happy. Some of us believe if we ignore that little nagging feeling when our true selves are trying to push forward into the light of day it will go away. It won't go away. It will keep trying to come out and the harder you resist the harder your life will get. Ask yourself what it will take to make you feel safe. Make sure it's reasonable. Allow yourself to dream of a life unknown to you, allow yourself to dream of being a happy homeowner on your own and very soon.

Hard questions to ask yourself:
- Am I really scared or have I been taught to be afraid?
- Who is teaching me to be afraid?
- Do they know me better than I know myself?
- What negative thoughts am I allowing to cloud my vision?
- What is the worst that could happen?
- What options would I have to help me deal with that?

Telling yourself, "I'm fine as I am, I don't want any more than this"

If this is something you say, you are deluding yourself. You don't want to know the truth and you won't allow yourself to dream because you are afraid to get hurt by dreaming too big. You believe the limitations you have set for yourself and you won't let your soul, your inner child come out to play. You may have been told not to expect more, to be happy with what you have. Sure, go ahead and give thanks for all of the blessings in your life, pay homage to them all. You need to do this regularly. And then set a big-ass goal and go get it. If you are renting a nice place and you save a bit of money each year and make a couple of bucks on stocks you may tell yourself you are fine with that because deep down you are afraid to achieve more success. You deserve more, you can have it all. Don't let them bring you down by internalizing those harsh restrictive beliefs that you can only have so much and that it is bad to want more. When the thing comes to you it may not look like what you are envisioning in your mind but it's already out there for you to go get. See the opportunities around you. Know what it is you truly want and go get it.

Hard questions to ask yourself:
- What would happen if I allowed myself to really dream?

- What are my beliefs about money?
- Do I believe I will become evil when I have an abundance of money?
- Will I walk all over people when I have money?
- Do I do that now? If not, why would that change when I have abundance?
- What would I ask for if I had all the resources at my fingertips with absolutely no restrictions?

Preaching, "I choose health over wealth. You can't have both"

Yes, you can. Rich people know they can have everything they want, that they can have health, wealth, and happiness. Poor people choose one or the other because they limit themselves with a scarcity mindset. Adopt an abundance mindset and get everything you want.

Hard questions to ask yourself:
- Do I believe there is room in my life for health and happiness?
- Do I believe I can be wealthy and happy?
- Do I believe I can be heathy, wealthy, and happy?
- Do I believe I deserve to have a great life?
- Do I believe I would become ill if I became successful?
- Do I believe the universe is abundant and there is enough for all my desires?
- Am I limiting yourself? If so, how can I change that?

Trying to wait for the perfect time

You believe you can time the real estate market and you are going to wait for the perfect time. You can't time the market. When the time is right for you to buy a home and you have the means to do it, then the time is right. The real estate market can change overnight and by the time you hear about it in the media it will be one or two months later. Waiting for the perfect time in your life doesn't work either. You'll wait until the kids grow up, or you'll wait until you get a better job, or you'll wait until you're married, or wait until you have more money. There is a strong disconnect with how you will actually feel when those things happen, e.g. you have more money. You may believe that you will feel more secure and it will be easier but the opposite could be true. You might be less likely to part with your money, you've grown accustomed to seeing that big number in your bank account and you will have a hard time spending it on your home or investment property. You probably already have enough money now especially if you have more than five per cent saved as a down payment for your home. Circumstances like interest rates could change for the worse, pushing your dream out of reach. Will you actually save enough money to make a huge difference or should you buy now and still save plus earn equity in your investment? How will inflation affect the value of your savings? If you wait for everything to be perfect you'll die waiting. You are simply wishing; you are not goal setting. Tap into your reasons why and carpe diem!

Hard questions to ask yourself:
- What will happen if I don't do it now?
- What is really holding me back? How am I rationalizing?
- What is it that I am waiting to happen? Is this reasonable?
- If it were to happen after I had purchased my home what would be the worst possible outcome?
- How would I deal with that?
- How do I deal with challenges?
- Do I really believe that I can predict the future one year from now, three years, five years, 10 years from now?

Moving will be such a hassle

You will have to go to the bank, change your mailing address with everyone, get utilities hooked up, pack and pack and pack, clean, purge, you'll have to deal with success and therefore deal with change so it just doesn't seem worth it. Oh the hits just keep on coming! Your egoic mind is like the battery-operated bunny who never quits. It will try to wear you down with such nonsense and soon you will believe that going to bank is going to be such a big hassle that you decide to just keep renting until you run out of money. The fear-based ego makes that sound like a good idea, but you can see that it isn't good at all.

Write this stuff down, ladies. This is easy to overcome if you are aware in advance that nonsense like this will come up in your head and could cause you to abandon even your most important goals. Early on in your home buying journey write down every negative thought that comes into your head and then shine light on it and really take a good look at it in order to determine what it is. It will most likely be an old deep-rooted negative belief that you have allowed to run your life up until now and it's time to kick it to the curb and replace it with the opposite and right belief. When you are close to making your home purchase and this dumb thought comes up again, review your notes and get into the right way of thinking and believing in yourself. Control your mind or it will control you.

Hard questions to ask yourself:
- Is achieving a goal a burden or a win?
- Will a minor inconvenience that will pass quickly cause you to stay where you are indefinitely?
- Can I enlist help that will allow me to deal with the inconveniences more easily or with less effort?
- If I am able to enlist help but I refuse to, and I in turn abandon my goal, am I rationalizing?
- Does it make sense to abandon my goal because of these small inconveniences?

You want to believe the naysayers, the media that always reports doom and gloom

The media sells fear and often spin statistics to scare us into believing the real estate market is not a good place to invest your hard-earned money. The naysayers may mean well but are stealing your dream just the same. Stop following the media, stop reading the blogs that spew fear, avoid engaging with negative people. Surround yourself with positivity. Believe in yourself. Set your goal and remain true to your goal. You will surprise yourself with what you can achieve if you go about it the right way.

Hard questions to ask yourself:
- Am I looking for a way out?
- Why am I looking for a way out instead of working toward my goal? Do I want to achieve my goal?
- How will I feel once I have achieved my goal?
- How would I feel if I were to abandon my goal?
- What would my life look like if I gave up on my goal?
- What is it going to take to make me feel safe?

Making it more difficult than it needs to be

We do this by over analyzing every detail, trying to find every angle, trying to predict every little thing that could happen, thinking you can do it privately without the help of a professional network, stretching out the amount of time it takes, which allows all of your fears to come back with a vengeance. As soon as an obstacle comes up you allow it to derail your dream or you create an obstacle by making the goal impossible to achieve, e.g. offering $400,000 on a $500,000 property and then saying it wasn't meant to be. That's not a case of divine intervention, that's a case of capitalism. We worry over things that don't really matter, worry about every scenario that could happen years down the road and don't trust ourselves to be able to deal with it. The best way you can control your circumstance is to not try to control everything about it. Create your best self, create your best life. Create and achieve your dream.

Hard questions to ask yourself:
- What is the emotion that is driving this desire to over analyze?
- What is behind my refusal to accept the data that supports the property value?
- Why am I purposely sabotaging myself?
- What do I really want?
- How am I justifying my actions?

How to Set and Achieve Your Goal of Home Ownership

Step 1: Set a Goal

In a previous chapter, you were asked to focus on why you want to buy a home. You made a list of reasons and dug deep into your understanding to help you determine the root of the desire. It's time to refresh your memory by reviewing the list.

Sit or relax in a quiet calm space and read your list out loud to yourself. As you read, you will find that you resonate with one or two reasons on your lists. Allow yourself to become emotional about the reason or reasons why you want to own your home.

Get into the emotions of it and really allow yourself to feel them

Once you are able to feel the desire you must write on a fresh page of paper very clearly what your intent is. Be specific with your language and always keep the language positive. Avoid writing what you don't want, always focus on what you really want. Get into it, write what you see when you envision your new home. Visualize yourself in your new home, how do you feel, what do you look like, what does the space feel like? Write out the emotions you will feel once you accomplish your goal and you are living in your new home. In your vision, imagine how grateful you will feel. Imagine how you will use the space, what your furniture will look like, what the neighbourhood feels like. Feel the bliss. Write as much detail as you can. If there is a specific building or complex you want to live in, add the details.

Visualize yourself in your new home
How long will you give yourself to achieve the goal? Choose a date and be specific. Write the month, day, and year.

Write out your projected date to acquire the property
In order to achieve your goal are you willing to work for it, to make sacrifices of time and energy and perhaps a vacation away? Are you willing to budget, ask for a raise, perhaps leave your comfort zone and apply for a better paying job? Are you willing to stretch yourself to enable the growth required to achieve your goal? Are you willing to put a large chunk of your income each week or month into your bank account, and if so how much money? Write out on the page what you are willing to give in order to get your new home, as long as it is moral, ethical, and legal.

Write out what you will give to get this
Set a plan on how to achieve this goal. You don't have to know all the steps right now, but you already know some of them and you can write them out.

Set a plan
What actions can you take to get you closer to your goal today? It can be as simple as reaching out to a mortgage consultant to discover what your borrowing power is today and how to improve it if need be. You could open a separate bank account to use for building your down payment, research the RRSP advantages for home buyers, or reach out to a real estate professional. You could start surfing on real estate websites. Write out three steps you can take this week to get you closer to your goal.

Take action immediately

When you become inspired, have an idea pop into your head, or come up with a creative way to resolve an issue or to overcome and obstacle act on it immediately. You must act as soon as the idea pops into your head. If the idea is to visit a neighbourhood to get a feel for the vibe, do it on your way to work or during your lunch break or after work today. As soon as you can, act. This is where many dreams die, right here. You may have a great plan worked out but if you don't take action it's nothing but a bunch of words on a piece of paper or a device. Without action your dream, your goal, your vision is a lovely story you tell yourself, delude yourself with. Act now. I'm not kidding.

Think creatively and act immediately

Create a concise statement using the information above. This is your goal. It should contain what you want, when you want it buy, what you plan to give to get it, your plan and actions. Keep writing and tweaking until you nail it. You'll know once you've nailed it because it feels different, it feels right, it may feel a little scary but that's all right. When you strive toward a goal you are leaving what you know and reaching for something bigger and better. That can be a little uncomfortable or a lot uncomfortable, but go for it. Embrace the challenge, embrace your dream, embrace your power.

Create a clear concise statement

At this point, you can take some time to sit quietly and just reflect on what you have written. Record yourself saying it out loud and play it on a loop if you can. Memorize it. I like to meditate with my statement. Become aware of your feelings when you hear it or say it. You may not believe it yet, but keep at it. I had been meditating on my goal statement and noticed a little twinge of something, and suddenly realized that the twinge had been there the day before and possibly for some time before that. I stopped and shed light on it. I wanted to know what it was. It was a fear, and a ridiculous one at that. I was afraid that when I achieved my goal people would hate me or stop liking me. I had already experienced this phenomenon at various times in my life and been able to deal with it. So I simply dismissed the fear as being ridiculous and having no legs and released it. It never came up again, it was gone. It's important for you to be in tune with your feelings as you sit calmly and review your goal statement. As negative thoughts appear simply dismiss them, don't own them. Soon they'll stop coming altogether if you keep up this work.

Review and memorize your goal

Step 2: Repeat, Auto-suggestion

You might have a bit of trouble believing that you can actually achieve your goal and that's okay, don't quit. The best way to build the belief is to use auto-suggestion or self-hypnosis. This is accomplished very easily by repeating aloud your goal statement many times each day. You can record your voice on your smartphone and play it back to yourself while you drive, cook, get ready for work, meditate, work out, dance, relax, and so on. Post it on your mirror where you get ready every morning, on your refrigerator, as a screen saver . . . anywhere and everywhere. The idea is to give this goal top of mind awareness. It should never leave your mind completely. You should never say, "Oh yeah, I forgot I'm working on a goal" because it should always be running in the background if not the foreground of your mind. Think of having a variety of apps open on your smartphone that you are not actively using at this moment. Unless you take the steps to close them they are always running in the background. That's what you should aim for with your goal statement, to have it always open and active. By doing so your mind will be open to the multitude of possibilities around you.

Repeat your goal many times each day
You'll notice things that you had never noticed before but were always there. You'll see FOR SALE signs all over the place, condo buildings that you never really paid attention to and real estate advertisements that had always been there but you never noticed. This is because your goal of home ownership is constantly running in the background. It is crucial

that this happens and in order for it to happen you just have to repeat your goal statement many times each day. As you do so you will find that you truly begin to believe that you can achieve your goal. Let this goal become an obsession for you.

Keep the goal top of mind

It's okay to tweak the goal as you do this, as long as you don't talk yourself out of the goal. You can tweak as you go because you add more detail to your dream or get more specific on some aspect of the goal, but you must never abandon your goal of home ownership.

While you are calmly repeating your goal statement, you may notice negative thoughts come up quite strongly. If you wish to write them down each day in a journal you will soon find that your fears are coming to mess you up. Take a look at them and ask yourself if they are true. Do you deserve to be a homeowner? Of course you do. Are you capable of achieving your goal? Yes, 100 per cent yes. Should you? YES! What if Mr. Right comes along?

So what?

Review and tweak the goal as needed

"What if" can be a dream as in, "What if I could buy a house in my favourite neighbourhood?" If that is your thought, act on it immediately by taking the steps outlined here in how to set your real estate goal. "What if" can be negative as in "What if I lose my job?" Look at your "what if" list and develop the self-confidence you need to overcome any obstacle that comes your way. Sydney lost her job twice while she was a homeowner and took steps to ensure that she came out ahead, and you can too. Because you control your thoughts you can choose to allow the "what if" list to hold you back if you really want to or you can choose to soar to heights beyond what you can dream. Control your thoughts in a way that allows you to achieve your goal.

Control your thoughts

It's usually frowned upon to write out the negative thoughts you have but in this case I like to encourage it so that you can respond to each one while you are calm and rational. When you write, "What if Mr. Right comes along?" you will follow up with the reasons why that will not stop you from pursuing and achieving your dream of home ownership. If Mr. Right comes along and he is threatened by your accomplishment he isn't Mr. Right at all. Mr. Right loves and respects you for who you really are and that is a powerful, self-confident goal achiever. By achieving your goal you will attract the right kind of partner who will admire and love you for who you are and home ownership is not going to make anyone less attractive or less worthy of love. That would be ridiculous! Recognize this fear and all of your fears as old beliefs from the past that do not serve you well. Now take that list of negatives and on a separate page write out the opposite and positive belief.

Replace your false and negative beliefs with the truthful positive ones
What if you lose your job? It would be frightening, and it could cause much anguish and anxiety until you are able to replace your income. It wouldn't be any less frightening if you were paying $2,400 in rent though, would it? At least when you own your home you have options just like the woman from the furniture store. You might be able to pull out equity to live off, you could rent out some or all of your home and move elsewhere, you could sell the property to relieve the burden of payments and to cash in on any profit. All the while you would be networking and actively finding a way to replace your lost income, if you needed to. This too is an obstacle that you will be able to overcome if it ever came to be. You would be strong enough and confident enough in yourself to be able to deal with it. How do I know? Because you were able to set the goal of home ownership and you achieved it, so you now have winning consciousness. You completed what you started, you are success conscious. You are unbeatable!

Practise winning and adopt success consciousness

Step 3: Support and Persistence

Now it is time to find people who will support your dream. It may not be your family and friends. If you recall, Sydney enlisted the help of her trusted realtor for the support she needed in order to achieve her goal. She knew her mother did not believe she could or should buy her own home, so she did not involve her in the process and did not share her wins or concerns with her. She simply placed her trust in her realtor to guide her home. She did not share her goal with her co-workers or friends as she knew that there would be naysayers who would try to hold her back even without knowing they were doing so.

You can share your goal with people who have done it recently and who you know will encourage you to overcome objections, who believe in the power of home ownership and who wholeheartedly want you to succeed. If you don't find anyone who checks these boxes just rely on your professionals, your mortgage consultant, and your licensed full-time trustworthy realtor.

Find like-minded people for support

The strongest support comes from within and you can access the support by recommitting to your goal every single day. During this time you will commit to your decision to buy property and with decision comes determination. You may experience setbacks but with determination you will be able to forge ahead toward your goal undeterred for any length of time. You may have to have a little meltdown for a moment or two but that's it. Deep breath in, wipe your tears, look yourself in the mirror, and recommit to your goal. Make the decision to succeed and become determined to overcome whatever hurdle you are facing and to move forward. No setback is too big, you are a winner. You've got this.

Recommit to your goal

If the setback is something that forces you to use your imagination to overcome an obstacle or to tweak your plan a bit you can do it. Look for opportunities and if you don't find them create them.

Look for and create opportunities

Do not quit and do not forget exactly what is motivating you to buy. Read your WHY list again, reconnect with the passion and use it to strengthen your resolve. Remember when Narissa wanted a place to display her beloved books and she had in mind a den or second bedroom? Her budget would not accommodate the extra space within her preferred neighbourhood. I showed her that the bedroom was extra-long offering plenty of wall space for display units, built-ins, or shelves to satisfy her longing to showcase her books. She was not open to the opportunity and would not consider it and eventually quit pursuing her goal. Remember when I wanted to be on a racetrack with my idol and I pictured it differently than the opportunity that presented itself? I jumped at the opportunity with joy and to this day I marvel at how that ever happened.

Review your WHY often and connect to the emotion

Your support group may be able to help you with this point. They may be more open to the opportunities than you are because they are more objective. Tweaking doesn't mean quitting, it means accepting 75 per cent as good enough when you just can't get it all or if it doesn't look exactly how you had imagined. Your support group will help you see clearly when it's time to hold out for more and when it's time to accept the opportunity right in front of you. Choose your support group wisely, like Ciara and Alannah both did, and you may find it easier to succeed.

Allow your support group to direct you toward opportunity

Step 4: Determination

Be persistent, don't give up as soon as the obstacles arise. Look at Sydney, that powerhouse who had to renovate while living elsewhere for six full months and lost her job twice while being a homeowner. She didn't give up, she was persistent and achieved her goal. Her advice to women is to know yourself and to know how to face a challenge, be optimistic and don't listen to the naysayers. Believe in yourself, push yourself. Fatima was determined to get a condo of her own and her desire was so strong that she did not quit. She persisted, she lived in dark spider-ridden basements so that she could heal, build herself up again, save money and build her career to the point where she could comfortably purchase a home. She wasn't going to let anything stand in her way. For her to be successful she had to be open to opportunities and dropped the idea of owning an expensive parking spot, choosing to rent a spot for her car. It gave her the opportunity to purchase her dream home within her budget. It was a creative solution to her problem and since her dream was home ownership and not to own a parking spot in Toronto she was able to refocus and win. Even though she has moved out and rented it to a tenant, she is so happy with her condo she gives the advice that one must not let go of their dream, to know it's for you and you have to have it.

Be determined and persistent

You must envision yourself beyond the finish line and on the podium if you want to win. Athletes do it all the time and if they can't see themselves winning they don't win. After Serena, the younger of the Williams sister tennis stars won the first Grand Slam for either of them Venus admitted that she didn't know how to win or close out a match, how to fight. Venus said, "It was a defining moment based on how you were going to react. Are you going to learn from her example or are you going to crumble?" Venus chose to learn and went on to win four more championships before Serena won another. Venus is reported to say that Serena taught her how to win that day.

Get used to the feeling of home ownership in your dream and you will get it in real life. Emily could not feel the emotion attached to winning strongly enough to help her overcome the fears that cropped up. She had been focused on the wrong thing, and it was easy for her to sabotage herself. Had she spent hours, days, and months visualizing herself in her new home she would have become more determined to achieve her goal and less likely to crumble.

Envision yourself after the win

Step 5: WIN!

Get it and enjoy the win. You've accomplished something big, your worthy goal. Now that you have trained yourself how to win you can use that new knowledge to achieve many more wonderful things for yourself. Take some time to pat yourself on the back for a while. Don't get too comfortable, you'll be setting a new goal soon and you'll strive toward the most wonderful things you can imagine.

CHAPTER 16

Some Final Words

To become aware, you have to break out of the automaton mode. When you take the same way home each day you seem to get home without even trying; you can't remember if you had to stop at a red light at the intersection down the street. You don't remember what the houses and buildings looked like on the way home. If I asked you if you saw the red brick house on a certain street you would most certainly not, unless you were looking for a house on that street, or unless the house had something special about it that had attracted your consciousness. Otherwise, you could drive by it every day without noticing it. I joke that if I don't set the GPS for the grocery store I will forget that I need to stop there on the way home, I'll end up in my driveway before I recall that I was going to get groceries. It's kind of frightening to think that we drive this 3,000-pound vehicle while we ourselves are on autopilot. If you want to become more present you have to change things up a bit. Take a new way home one day and you will be more present and more aware of your surroundings.

Use the same idea with your own actions and language. Become aware of how you act, what the triggers are and what you say about yourself and about everything. Write down the things you say to yourself. Are they kind? Do they help you achieve your dreams? Or are they limiting? What happened to make you say those things to yourself? Where were you, who were you with, what language did you hear?

Once you have written a few things down you will begin to be able to identify the trigger and the belief. You can make the decision to change it if it does not serve you well. Awareness is the first element of change. Become aware of your conditioned response, observe it and decide whether you will keep it or replace it with something better. Feel the power of delving into the clutter of your mind and begin sorting, organizing and deleting any negative ideas that hold you back. Think of life like a big sociology experiment. When someone or something triggers you, choose to become an observer and choose not to react. Most times, it's them not you. What I mean is, it's their issue, their conditioning, and it has little to do with you. Just remember that and you will find it easier to slip into the observer's shoes. You'll be calmer and see the situation for what it really is and the answer may become clear to you in those moments. In the past you may have gone off, cried, reacted in fear or anger or hidden in your shell, but as an observer with a new perspective you will be able to cut through the noise, see clearly what is happening and pick your battles.

You already possess everything you need, no matter how old or young you are. The power, the ability to choose, the ability to see opportunity is in you and is not in the circumstances. The timing is right, don't play the game of getting ready to get ready.

Look inside and learn what created your perception and change it immediately. Don't dwell on the past, leave it where it is, focus on your new reality and you will instantly discover your new plan and your new direction. The opportunity to change is right now. Take it.

Go for it, Babe. You got this.
Sandra

How to change the paradigms

Become aware of yourself and be true to yourself.
1. Recognize the paradigm
2. Create an affirmation of the exact opposite
3. Repeat it frequently

Techniques to overcome fear

There are many notable techniques that are available to people who would like some help overcoming fear or changing paradigms. Here are a few for you to research:
- Tapping
- Neurolinguistic Programming (NLP)
- Hypnotherapy
- Auto-suggestion, auto-hypnosis
- Essential oils for calm and clarity and manifesting
- Visit sandrarinomato.com for resources and recommendations
- Coherence breathing

Goal Setting Formula

1. Develop a SMART goal: specific, measurable, attainable, relevant, and timely
2. What you will give to get it
3. Date

4. Plan
5. Statement
6. Repetition/visualization

To Do List

- Quit the habit of quitting, finish everything you start
- Become success conscious vs failure conscious
- Focus on your desire, not hope, not wishful thinking
- Burn the bridges that don't serve you
- Be determined and not swayed by opinion or obstacles
- Visualize often while you are in the zone
- Open your mind to believe, drop the paradigms, open door, faith
- Repetition of your goal statement
- Auto-suggestion
- Dominating thoughts should be about wanting to buy a home
- Attach emotion to the goal
- Demand persistence of yourself
- Develop self-confidence
- Love the world, love all people, in a manner that is for the highest good
- See yourself past the finish line and on the podium
- Be on alert for opportunity and act immediately
- Refresh your commitment by reading your WHY a few times per week and before you go looking at homes
- Do the work, i.e. credit check, save money, clear up debt
- Be with people who are in harmony with your goal
- Hire the pros

Cheat Sheet: Goal to Buy Real Estate

- Become aware of your paradigms, especially those around self-worth
- Change the limiting beliefs with autosuggestion
- Fix your mind on what you want (not what you don't want)
- Write out your detailed WHY
- Work on it until you feel it
- What will you give up (i.e girls trip, get part time job, ask for raise, clear debt)
- Set a date to achieve it
- Write it out
- Visualize it often with you as homeowner, you are inside your home
- Get the plan (e.g. down payment, mortgage approval, area)
- Act on it: open account, get your credit report, qualify now for mortgage with a pro, and ask what steps you need to take to get one
- Repetition, recommit to the goal, dream
- Enlist the help of a realtor
- Be determined, don't let obstacles stop you
- Read your WHY again
- Seize opportunities
- Offer a price that will actually get you the place
- Accept the deal
- Move in
- Celebrate with family and friends

ABOUT THE AUTHOR

Toronto real estate Broker/Owner and former host of the popular HGTV shows *Property Virgins* and *Buy Herself*, Sandra Rinomato, has over 25 years of experience in one of the toughest markets in Canada. She has worked with hundreds of clients, many of them single women, and understands the importance of first knowing yourself well, setting goals, remaining flexible, and keeping the goal of home ownership front and centre in your thinking. She lives in Toronto with her husband and business partner Gary MacRae and her two stepsons Cody and Albert. Their beloved and very photogenic Nessie, the Old English Sheepdog, completes the family.